Ruanidh Ormiston
Newtonmore Riding Centre
07831 338012

RHAS 2010

Discover Off-Road Riding

With best wishes for
your off-road adventures ~

Love Godfrey

Bronagh. C. Staren

Kate Godfrey and Shonagh Steven BHSII

Illustrated by Mark Weallans
Photography by Caroline Heard

Discover Off-Road Riding

A Practical Guide

Alight Publishing

© Kate Godfrey and Shonagh Steven
First published in Great Britain 2010

ISBN 978-0-9565911-0-4

Alight Publishing
Inverquiech
Alyth
BLAIRGOWRIE
Perthshire PH11 8JR

CONTENTS

Foreword

The days have long gone when knowledge was handed down through the generations. The internet, our modern equivalent, does not always give hands-on experience to enable the rider to tackle a variety of situations.

This book fills a huge gap and is an absolute 'must read' for riders of every level who wish to get full enjoyment from their horse while exploring the countryside.

Packed with practical, common sense solutions to problems which you may encounter, Discover Off – Road Riding will provide you with the knowledge and confidence to embark safely on longer rides and more adventurous off-road challenges.

An amusing and easy read, it is full of information and attention to detail which will inspire every rider to have a go at off- road riding.

Loraine Young

Chairman, BHS Scotland

Off-Road Riding — What's That About?

For centuries mankind has used horses to travel across country: for droving cattle and sheep, trading goods, carrying ore from mines, military purposes or travelling from one religious centre to another. Even in the twenty-first century, many of these tracks remain as a legacy for today's riders to enjoy, increasingly protected by legislation and by the efforts of access campaigners.

In an age of jet engines and super-fast broadband connections, this old-fashioned method of travel is inspiring a new generation of riders to explore the countryside on horseback at their leisure – to enjoy nature, to explore areas which they would miss hurtling by in a car, or just to spend time with their horse or pony without the pressure of competition.

It's an excellent way of challenging yourself and your horse while improving his training and fitness, and of developing the close bond which can only come from long hours in each other's company. It keeps a riding club horse relaxed, keen and fit, and the idlest of ponies generally develops a new zest for work on seeing some new horizons. It's rare to find a horse which doesn't appear to relish a bit of exploration - providing he has been properly prepared.

For the purposes of this book, off-road riding covers travelling with your horse across country, following a route you have devised on tracks or paths, at a pace which suits you both (but which will mostly be slower than the pace of, say, competitive endurance riders.) The distance you cover, and the speed you go at, are immaterial – what's important is that you – and your horse - enjoy it! Some riders describe it as 'equine backpacking' or 'horse rambling'.

It's a good way of sharing your interest with your family, a friend or partner, even if they don't ride themselves - we know quite a few couples where one will mountainbike or walk while the other rides, meeting up at a pre-arranged camping spot or a bed and breakfast. You can also combine it easily with another interest of your own such as photography, drawing or simply observing wildlife.

You can do it at any level of challenge you like. Some riders will thoroughly enjoy a day ride round some new territory with a few friends: others may be dreaming of following one of the increasing number of long-distance routes promoted for equine use, or of riding from coast to coast, or from John O Groats to Land's End. Perhaps you have had a go at endurance, pleasure rides or Le Trec, and would like to go it alone, or perhaps you just fancy doing something different with your horse in a new location. Whatever your aspirations, this book is designed to help you achieve your goals.

Why this book?

We are *passionate* about off-road riding. Our huge enthusiasm for enjoying outdoor adventures with all the fun horses we have trained and ridden, and the wonderful expeditions we have had, rubs off on other riders we meet. It must do, because they say, "I would SO love to do that!" However, much to our sadness, this is often quickly followed up with "But..." Some of the 'buts' include:

- I don't know where I can ride

- What if we get lost?

- Do I need permission?

- I don't think my horse would be fit enough

- I don't think *I* would be fit enough

- My horse doesn't like...crossing water/cows/

  tractors/whatever!

- I don't think my horse would behave himself

- I wouldn't dare get off – I'd never get back on

- I wouldn't know what to take with me...

They *can* do it - and so can you. The aim of this book is to help you train and prepare your horse - and yourself - for enjoyable and safe off-road riding, whether that is a circular day ride with a few chums, or disappearing into Britain's wild places for several days with a tent.

That is the purpose of this book: to share with you what we have learned about riding through unfamiliar countryside, coping with common hazards, what you need to take with you, how to train and care for your travelling companion and what to do if things go wrong.

The Ideal Travelling Companion

1

"The perfect horse has never been foaled..."

Perhaps you are in the enviable position of currently looking for a horse to buy as your equine travelling companion, and this chapter details what, ideally, you will be looking for.

More likely, you already have a horse or pony who may have some behavioural or physical issues you would like to work on to develop him into a safe, fit and happy equine.

Don't despair if he's currently closer to 'Sam' than 'Amy' though (see following pages). There's plenty of help for him (and you) in this book: often horses will miraculously improve with consistent work and handling, not to mention some fresh horizons.

Sometimes it's about making the most of what you've got: for off-road riding, a horse or pony which is sound and enthusiastic (preferably with brakes, too) can still give you endless pleasure, while you're improving the rest of him.

Fancy trying off-road riding?

Not every horse is completely suitable – which would you prefer, Sam or Amy?

Snorting Sam...

Refuses to stand still for mounting;

Is disobedient and unreliable in traffic;

Spooks wildly at real or imagined hazards, often unseating his rider;

Fusses, frets and sweats up when anywhere he doesn't know, exhausting both himself and his rider;

Threatens and kicks out at other horses on a ride;

Insists on going first in a group – at which point he slows down to a stop;

Is difficult to manoeuvre at gates or other obstacles;

Naps towards other horses, the trailer or home;

Bucks at the bumping of saddlebags or tree branches which brush him;

Refuses to cross water, bridges or white markings on the road;

Won't allow another horse to be led off him, or to be led by a rider on another horse;

Either pulls like a train, or refuses to go forward without huge expenditure of energy from his rider;

Won't stand quietly when tied;

May or may not load into the box at the end of a ride!

Angelic Amy...

Stands stock still to be mounted and will stand without being held for short periods;

Goes forward quietly, confidently and willingly in unfamiliar country;

Responds to her rider's weight aids and moves away promptly from her rider's leg to manoeuvre round obstacles or traffic hazards;

Will remain at the pace her rider has set, even on a loose rein, without trying to either emulate the Derby winner or need constant kicking to keep her in a trot;

Will pick her way with care on a loose rein through water, or across soft or stony ground;

Will walk easily beside her rider without barging off, trying to eat grass or lagging behind, and will follow directly behind her leader Indian file without treading on his heels or running her over where the path is narrow;

Will look – or even stop – when she sees something unfamiliar, but will walk on when reassured;

Is polite with other horses;

Waits for her rider when she falls off!

Most of us who are neither teenagers nor masochists would probably prefer their horse to be closer to Amy's end of the spectrum. Let the journey begin...

While virtually any sound and reasonably sane horse can be used for off-road riding, there are some sensible pointers to consider, whether you are purchasing a new horse or considering trying it out on one you already have. These are pointers only: we personally know of three horses which have the insurance stamp 'L' (for Loss of Use) which have gone on to cover thousands of trouble-free miles with their new riders – but, on the whole, it's better not to look for trouble. With horses, the trouble so often finds you!

The good news is that you can afford to be flexible: things which would make a horse unsuitable for the show ring such as old scarring, a common head or old but healed injuries are irrelevant for an off-road rider where handsome is definitely as handsome does. You will be spending a lot of time with this horse, so, in the old adage, 'is he a horse you can live with'? If he is, the most important points to consider in an off-road horse (but by no means the only ones) are:

size; back; feet and brain.

We do recommend you have a British Veterinary Association five-stage vetting on any potential horse for purchase: it may seem like an added expense, but it's cheaper and less troublesome than keeping your lame horse on box rest for months, wondering if he'll ever come sound. At the very least, the vetting may throw up potential weaknesses or old injuries which will affect how you train and condition the horse, and will flag up any concerns about his heart or eyesight. If you decide to go ahead with the purchase, the vet's report may well help you to negotiate a better price to reflect the additional time it will take to condition him or costs of extra therapy. Be sure the vet carrying out the examination knows what you propose to do:

The horse will be ridden for long periods, not necessarily very fast

(you don't require a candidate for the Golden Horseshoe endurance ride)

The terrain may be very variable – stony, steep, boggy, roadwork

The horse will be required to keep condition, even on variable grazing.

By being observant, you can carry out a number of checks yourself to see if he's worth considering seriously before you commit to a vetting. Ideally you will have an instructor or experienced friend with you – they may spot something you don't.

This is your chance to assess him critically, look at his good points and his weaker points. The vast majority of horses can be improved by correct work and care, but only if you have the skills (and support if necessary) to do it. The more you expect of your horse as an athlete the more you need to look for conformational soundness and a trainable temperament.

17

Size DOES matter

Is the horse the right size for you? Because the build of horses varies so much, this is not necessarily his height in hands (even if the sellers have been accurate with this, which they often aren't.) Like Goldilocks, you are looking for the perfect fit – you're going to spend a lot of time up there.

Too big?

Unless you're planning to ride across the Mongolian desert, you are going to be mounting and dismounting A LOT. If you can vault on to a 16.3 horse like Frankie Dettori, this may not be an issue for you, but for most of us less athletic mortals, a horse which we can get on without borrowing our brother's climbing gear is preferable (as well as being kinder on the horse.) There are other issues which sometimes go along with bigger horses too: they may require more feeding (could be an problem on multi-day rides); they may require a bigger trailer; their increased weight may make them more prone to leg, foot, and musculo-skeletal problems; they may be less nimble on tricky ground. Can you comfortably reach to tack him up and fasten saddlebags?

If you are a bigger or heavier rider, don't assume that a big horse necessarily means a strong horse: he may be weak in the back and only really suitable for a lightweight rider. If you're a small person, do you have the strength to control him, both on the ground and while mounted? Whilst we know riding and handling horses should not be about strength *per se*, you still need to feel comfortable and in control.

Too small?

Assuming that the horse or pony is strong enough to carry you (see below), too small a horse can still cause you problems. A short neck (especially coupled with an upright shoulder) can lead to you feeling somewhat precarious up there, particularly if he's at all 'sharp'. If the horse is short-coupled, the saddle which fits him well may be too small for you, (especially if you have long thighs or a round bottom). Careful saddle-fitting can help this, but remember you may also need room for saddlebags.

Riding for a long time on a horse which is too small for your height can be tiring, as you have to work harder to keep your balance. If you ride a horse which appears too small for you, be prepared for comments from the public...

Too wide?

Some native ponies, native crosses and cob-type animals can have flat, broad backs with very little wither. While initially these feel comfortable and safe, after long days in the saddle you may feel very sore, particularly on the inside of your upper thighs or in your hips. Again, the right saddle can help (you may want to avoid broad, flat Western-type or treeless saddles, for example). There are also commercial 'hip-savers' available which are designed to alleviate this problem, but if you have short legs or any hip trouble, you may be better looking for a slightly narrower animal with more pronounced withers – or be prepared to do more walking!

Strong enough?

The difference between the type of riding described in this book and that of the average riding club horse is that you will be spending **much** more time on him. There are two traditional 'rules of thumb' which may help you decide if he will be able to carry you for long periods: bone and weight.

The 'bone' of a horse is a measurement which is taken round the leg just below the knee joint and is an indication of that horse's weight carrying capacity. A reasonable weight ratio is for a horse to carry 20% of his own body weight – and no, that doesn't mean a horse rippling with fat after three months at grass can carry a heavier rider.

A horse in reasonably fit condition weighing 500 kgs (1100lbs) should be able to carry a *maximum* weight of rider + saddle + gear weighing 100 kgs – that's 15 ½ stone.

It's not quite that simple in real life, of course. A heavier person may 'ride lighter' than someone who weighs considerably less if they are toned, balanced and support their own weight. There are other factors which can affect a horse's weight-carrying capacity, such as his age.

It is unfair to expect young horses or older horses to carry as much weight. Likewise a horse which is weak, recovering from injury or out of condition will require more fittening and correct muscling before being asked to carry *any* rider for long periods. A horse which has been allowed to go along gaily in an inverted frame for years is likely to have a weaker, concave back with poor muscle tone.

The traditional hunting 'weight' categories can be helpful when assessing your horse's weight–carrying potential:

Lightweight 8 ½" of bone means the horse can carry up to 12½ stone (175lbs/79.5kgs);

Middleweight 8 ½ to 9" of bone means the horse can carry up to 14 stone (196lbs/89kgs);

Heavyweight 9"+ of bone means he can carry over 14 stone. (Over 196lbs/89kgs)

These weights are for the rider fully clothed with boots on and including the saddle (not saddlebags though), and the horse is considered able to carry this for a full day's hunting.

Ideally his neck will arc upwards and forwards from the shoulder: a ewe neck or particularly weak neck is not advisable. Most off-road riders prefer a horse with a shorter back to a longer one: think of the difference between a compact humpbacked stone bridge and a dippy suspension bridge– and remember you sit right in the middle. When viewed from the side, does your horse look more like a square or a rectangle?

A concave, weaker back   **A shorter, stronger back**

The squarer, more compact horse with a 'leg at each corner' will find it easier to carry your weight, as well as finding it easier to collect and step under himself – the value of which will soon become obvious when you are riding down steep hills!

Compact square horses also often have two other very desirable traits: a broad chest (lots of heart and lung room) and strong, powerful hindquarters. Make sure the hips and hindquarters look level from behind - if not, they could be warning of an underlying problem. A short, well-muscled back also helps protect the sensitive area of the kidneys. As well as carrying you, your horse will be required to carry saddlebags.

Foot perfect?

Your farrier or vet will confirm to you that the vast majority of lameness occurs - or at least starts - in the horse's feet. While many feet can be improved by knowledgeable and sympathetic trimming, shoeing and nutrition, you want to start from the best possible baseline. Just as some people have thin hair, some horses have thin hoof walls! More than any other ridden horse, the off-road horse has to contend with stony or gravelly terrain – sometimes for hours on end. In addition, if your horse goes lame, you may be many miles from help. It can happen to any horse of course, but you are trying to minimise the risk.

Ideally, your horse will have matching pairs of front and back feet, since deformities can lead to stresses higher up the leg. Look at the feet from the front – do they seem like a pair? When you pick up the foot, is the area on each side of the frog equal in size and shape?

Your ideal horse will have good quality horn, dense and tough, without cracks or chipping. We tend to avoid horses with flat soles, as they are much more prone to bruising. Horses or ponies which have had laminitis in the past require extra-careful scrutiny – any suggestion of a dropped sole will make the horse unlikely to cope with the work ahead. Because this is such an important subject, Chapter 6 *Fitness and Care of the Off-Road Horse* looks at feet in much more detail.

The Foot

The horn quality and conformation of your horse's feet will have short and long term effects on the horse. Time, knowledge and a good farrier can help improve both horn quality and hoof balance. The horse has evolved over time to stand on one digit at the end of each limb giving him speed and agility. It does however mean that a lot of weight is supported on just one digit (the equivalent of our middle finger (front foot) and our middle toe (back foot). The foot not only bears the horse's weight but is also designed to reduce concussion and aid circulation.

The horn is the outer foot, protecting the inner sensitive parts. It bears most of your horse's weight and is also the structure to which the nails of the shoe are attached. The horn is made up of a similar structure to human hair and nails. Good horn is strong and does not break up easily, with a slightly shiny surface which helps controls moisture uptake and loss. Some horses naturally have good horn – a huge bonus.

Foot Balance

Hoof balance can be looked at in the way the foot makes contact with the ground and how it relates to the rest of the limb.

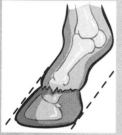

Front foot pastern angle should be 45 degrees with no breaks in angle.

Hind foot pastern angle should be 50 degrees with no angle breaks.

Front line view should be vertical with even amounts of foot on either side.

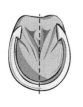

The sole should have the same distance from side to side as it does from the seat of corn to the toe. An imaginary line drawn down the centre of the hoof should show the same amount of hoof on either side.

Why worry?

Every time your horse's foot lands on the ground his pastern and foot absorbs much of the movement.

The back third of the foot expands and contracts with every footfall so if the foot is out of balance, misshapen or does not directly sit under the leg then one side will be taking much more of the concussion than the other, causing long term problems to cartilage and bone.

If his foot is not at the correct angle or does not match the angle of the pastern there is added wear on his tendons and joints.

Temper, temper

The horse's temperament can be summed up as his outlook on life, not necessarily his current behaviour – he can have an excellent temperament but lousy manners, if no-one has (yet) taught him differently. Just as we have different relationships with different people, the way we interact with individual horses can vary a great deal. You wouldn't want to go on holiday with someone who made you nervous, intimidated you, bored you, ignored you (or frequently bit you), would you? Perhaps luckily, we don't all like the same horses, just as we don't all like the same people. Only you can judge what is desirable (or at the very least acceptable) to you.

Off-road riders covering many miles often describe a bond with their horse which is like no other and comes from long hours in each other's company, facing challenges together, mutual trust, looking after each other (yes, many horses appear to have a sense of responsibility to their riders) and simply having a contented, interesting time together.

Bear in mind that steady, varied work within the horse's capabilities is likely to have a good influence on most. However, unless you are the sort of person who thrives on challenges, (and has good medical cover) you will probably think very carefully about choosing to spend many of your precious leisure hours in the company of:

- **Extremely nervous horses, especially if they have a strong flight mechanism and a tendency to bolt**

- **Overdominant horses which 'face you up' frequently**

- **Nappy horses**

- **Horses which do not interact well with others – a bore on the trail and a nightmare in camp**

- **Over–excitable, 'fizzy' horses which constantly want to be going faster**

- **Horses which get anxious or refuse to eat/drink in strange surroundings.**

It's not always easy to distinguish temperament from learned behaviour, especially if you don't know the horse. A horse which appears nervous or bolshy for example, may be quite different with another rider, or with more careful training. Likewise, the most willing and biddable of mounts can deteriorate rapidly with careless riding or unsympathetic handling.

If, like most riders at one time or another, you ultimately end up with a horse which is perhaps less than ideal, consider that he may be your greatest teacher and enable you to learn more about horses, off-road riding (and yourself) than you thought possible!

In order to learn effectively, you need to remain open-minded and sensible about what you ask the horse to do (in a safe environment to begin with), and for the time being at least, be content with small successes on which you can build.

The Ideal Travelling Companion

- is a horse you can get along with

- is the right size for you, without conformation defects which will affect his soundness

- has feet which will stand up to the work ahead

- has a trainable temperament

- is free from behavioural issues which will threaten your safety and ruin your enjoyment of your ride

Equipment 2

This chapter deals with the equipment you will need to start exploring the countryside on your horse. You may be relieved to find that certainly for shorter rides, you've probably got most of it already; either in your tackroom or around the house. Once you start doing longer journeys, using a packhorse, or camping, things can get a little more complicated. The good news is that with a little thought and ingenuity, you can generally acquire the things you need without too much additional expense.

Much of what you use is down to personal choice, but any equipment must be robust and well-maintained. Everything will have to work a lot harder than it does riding in an arena, and you may be a long way from home if a bridle or girth strap breaks. In addition, you may find yourself having to negotiate your way through a forest, through undergrowth or water and it's likely that sooner or later you (and your equipment) will get drenched! Trying to read a map which is rapidly transforming itself into a papier-mache clump is neither easy nor fun.

The other key aspect to consider is how well everything fits. Does it rub, pinch or chafe anywhere? By the time you've ridden 20 or 30 miles, possibly on steep terrain, any small problems will have been magnified many times, causing pain or discomfort to your horse (or you). Badly packed saddlebags bumping into your horse at every stride (up to 4,000 times every hour) are guaranteed to irritate or injure the most forgiving mount.

As with any sport or pastime, the best equipment is not necessarily the most expensive: it's what does the job for you. The following suggestions are based on our experience of what works (and as importantly, what hasn't worked), as well as input from other off-road riders, walkers, cyclist and campers. You should be prepared to be open-minded, and to experiment, until you find what best suits your particular needs.

Saddle

We are asked more often about saddles than any other item of equipment – and rightly so. This key piece of equipment is the single most important item to get right. A poorly-fitting saddle can easily result in long-term injury or behavioural problems in your horse: if you had to walk the Pennine Way in boots which were a size too small, you might start napping back towards the car park too!

As well as fitting the horse, the saddle must also fit *you*, and enable you to sit comfortably in a balanced position for hours at a time. If you constantly feel that the saddle is, for example, encouraging you to tip forward (as many do), you will quickly feel uncomfortable and fatigued.

There are several companies which specialise in saddles for endurance, distance riding and horse packing, and some suggestions given in Chapter 11 *Further Resources*. If you get really enthusiastic, sooner or later you will probably start lusting after one. Any well-fitting general purpose saddle will do to get you started, provided it meets the criteria outlined below. Forward cut jumping saddles are not really suitable because they are designed for the rider to ride with a short stirrup with the body inclined slightly forward to match that leg position. This is hard to sustain comfortably over many miles. However, a well-fitting jumping saddle is still preferable to an ill-fitting 'endurance' one!

Saddle fit

There is no substitute for having your saddle checked by a qualified professional – and remember that your horse may well change shape over time. However, there are several tests you can do yourself in the interim which will help you gauge if the saddle is suitable.

Saddle fit should be checked in three ways: visually with you standing on the ground; with a rider mounted, and with the horse in motion. With the saddle on the horse, loosely girthed and without the numnah, look at it critically. It should feel secure and 'in place', even with the girth loosely fastened. You should not be able to rock it backwards or forwards or from side to side with your hands.

Saddle Fit – Key Questions

- Too wide?
- Too narrow?
- Too long?
- Too short?
- Sufficient clearance at the shoulder blade?
- Sufficient clearance through the gullet?
- Level panel contact?

Saddle width

The saddle should appear to sit level in the seat (the part where the rider sits). If the saddle is too narrow at the front it will slope backwards causing a bigger percentage of the rider's weight to be carried at the back of the saddle. If the saddle is too wide at the front the seat will slope forward causing a bigger percentage of the rider's weight to be carried at the front. A good general rule is that you should be able to fit four fingers between the wither and the pommel without the riders weight and three with the rider mounted (or thereabouts).

Saddle length

If the saddle is too long it will press onto the loins. This is the sloping area in front of the highest point on the horse's hind quarters, and is a very sensitive area. If the saddle is too short it will concentrate the rider's weight on too small an area, which could lead to bruising.

Areas of Clearance:

Shoulder

With the horse's leg pulled forward you should be able to slide your hand easily between the side panels and the horse's skin from the pommel down to the girth. This checks that the horse has complete freedom of movement in his shoulder blades.

Gullet

Look through the saddle from pommel to cantle. When the girth is done up, you should be able to see daylight through the gullet. There must be clearance all the way along the spine: on a new saddle, this can be several inches, but even in a well-used saddle, there must be a least a couple of inches.

Panels

The panels can be checked from behind to make sure that they look level and they look as if the are making the same contact on each side of the spine. These panels should also feel smooth without any bumps or hollows when you run your hands over them when the saddle is off the horse. Remember, you should be able to slide your hand comfortably underneath the saddle along the shoulders. One of the key things to check for is that the saddle is not interfering with the shoulders - remember that these will rotate when the horse is actually in motion. A saddle which digs into the shoulders will, unsurprisingly, result in restricted movement (and possibly lots of other behavioural problems too).

To see examples of saddle fit, check out the photos on page 130.

Saddle fit when mounted

The saddle not only needs to fit the horse but also be comfortable and balanced for the rider. Usually we know whether we are comfortable almost straight away but here are a few things to look out for.

How the rider should feel...

- When seated in the saddle you should be able to fit your hand between your bottom and the cantle.

- You should be able to adjust your stirrups 2 or 3 holes without your knee going over the front of the knee rolls or feeling like you are being pushed out of the back of the saddle.

- You shouldn't feel the ridges at the side of the seat on the saddle under your thighs.

- You shouldn't feel like you are being pushed forwards on to the pommel.

- With your feet out of the stirrups close your eyes and ask yourself if you feel like you are tipping forwards or backwards. If it is the right saddle for you and the horse you should feel central, secure and balanced. (Photos taken of you will help identify this if you're not absolutely sure.)

- If you are relatively riding fit you shouldn't feel like you are straining to sit in the saddle and it definitely shouldn't hurt!

Whatever saddle you use, you might also like to consider adding a seat saver to add to your comfort on those long journeys. There are many types available: look for one which won't absorb water and be a soggy mess should you get caught in the rain.

The Talc Test

Dry patches on the horse's back after riding suggests either the saddle is bridging (not in contact with the horse) or the pressure is SO great that the horse cannot sweat in that area.

One simple way of testing for this is to cover the horse's saddle patch lightly with talc and then ride in the saddle (with no numnah). Take the saddle off and look at the panels underneath: does the talc evenly cover a wide area on both sides of the saddle? Areas where there is no talc shows the saddle isn't in contact here (known as 'bridging') which means that the rider's weight is unevenly distributed. If the talc coverage is much heavier on one side than the other, this can indicate unbalanced riding on your part, or that the horse's back muscles are unevenly developed. (Chapters 5 and 6 can help you with this, as can lessons with a good instructor. In more extreme cases, your horse may benefit from treatment from an equine back specialist).

 Photographs on page 128 show an example of good even talc coverage, and an example of problematic saddle fit.

When you dismount after working your horse, remove the saddle and run the *back* of your hand over the saddle area. (For most people, the back of the hand is more sensitive to temperature). Are there any 'hot spots'? These can indicate areas where the saddle is putting pressure on the horse's back.

Look carefully at the hair in the saddle area too – any areas where the hair is ruffled can indicate saddle movement or rubbing: uncorrected, this will result ultimately in hair loss or galling.

Stirrups and Leathers

While the stirrups you use for your normal riding will be perfectly adequate (you may like to add plastic or rubber treads for comfort), you may also like to explore the stirrups on the market which are specifically designed for long distance riding.

In general, these have wider treads and offer more comfort and support for your feet over a long period. Some also have shock-absorbing mechanisms which can be extremely helpful for riders who have a tendency towards knee or ankle pain when riding for long periods. Some of them feel quite bouncy though and take a bit of getting used to - much better to try them out at home first!

You might also like to explore the stirrups which are available with cages at the front - *essential* if you plan to ride in walking boots or if your saddle doesn't have safety stirrup bars. Should you come off, or your horse trip and fall in bad going, there is no danger of your foot getting trapped and you being dragged.

Many off-road riders prefer using Western-style fenders rather than traditional stirrup leathers, finding them more comfortable over long periods, especially if you don't wear chaps. Whichever stirrups you choose, they should always have 1 .5 cm space at either side of the rider's foot. *Always* check the stitching at the top of the stirrup leather and the wear where the leather creases round the iron. These are the two areas which often snap so BEWARE.

 See photograph on page 128 for an example of fenders with caged stirrups.

Pads and Numnahs

The use of a good saddle pad or numnah serves several purposes:

* To absorb sweat;
* To keep the underside of the saddle clean;
* For the horse's comfort, providing mild shock absorbtion;
* To protect the horse from saddlebags bumping against him;
* 'Grippy' pads can be useful for round-barrelled horses with no withers, to stop the saddle moving round especially when mounting;
* Compensate for *minor* saddle-fitting problems; eg on an older horse which will benefit from more protection either side of the spine.

Note that in some cases, padding can be positively detrimental. Thick padding (more than an inch) can *intensify* pressure - think of wearing thick socks and those too-small boots! It can also encourage the saddle to move, increasing friction and rubbing. A pad must always be easy to pull up into the saddle gullet, to allow free passage of air along the spine. It is vital that the front of the numnah does not slip down and press against the horse's withers. Numnahs that are shaped to stay up into the gullet are the best at avoiding this.

There are many types of saddle pad on the market, all with committed fans. Some riders swear by natural materials such as wool, which absorb sweat well (but can be achingly slow to dry); others prefer some of the newer high-tech materials which are often very quick to dry. A very experienced off-road rider we know swears by pads cut from a roll of Vetbed, which has kept her highly sensitive horse going without rubbing when nothing else seemed to work.

Whatever you decide to use, the pads must be kept clean (and watch out for detergent or soap residues - make sure they are thoroughly rinsed). Pads which can be turned upside down at lunchtime unsaddling are useful, as your horse can start the afternoon with a 'clean' pad. Some riders like wool blankets which can be refolded in a variety of ways, giving you four 'clean' sides - if you decide to try this, you must be very careful that the blanket is not wrinkling under the saddle and making your horse sore.

Bridle

Your usual bridle, provided it is well-fitting and doesn't rub, will be perfectly all right. You may want to consider removing the noseband - the fewer straps there are, the less chance of something rubbing. Likewise, select the mildest bit you can get away with.

Most parts on the bridle are adjustable. The browband is one piece which isn't and is often forgotten in the fitting process. The browband stops the bridle from falling back - it should not pull the bridle forward. You should be able to fit two fingers in the front of the browband. This will stop the bridle being pulled into the back of the horse's ear, which can be rather painful. Think of those sunglasses that didn't fit well and hit a nerve at the back of your ear and you'll know what the horse feels like when the browband doesn't fit! Ideally, none of your leatherwork, when correctly adjusted, will be on the top hole - if a strap breaks, it leave you nowhere to go.

When you get to the point of buying a new bridle, you might consider some of the synthetic endurance bridles, some of which convert quickly to a headcollar. Off-road riding often involves getting off to lead your horse or open a gate, or stopping to let him graze for a few minutes, so anything which makes this easy is a boon. Synthetic bridles can usually be washed in a washing machine, which may also be a selling point for you. However, they may not break as easily as a leather bridle in an emergency, so you may want to insert a 'breaking point' if it hasn't got one already.

Bitless bridles are currently popular, and they get rid of the need to remove the bit to let a horse graze comfortably on a ride. Some horses go extremely well in them, but you will want to be certain that you have brakes and steering firmly established *before* you venture out on a long ride, especially in company. Not all horses understand the pressure and release system of a bitless bridle straight away and therefore the rider should expect to have to do some re-training to help the horse understand. Some forms of bitless bridle can be very severe in their pressure so use with care.

Reins

Plain leather reins which are wet can be slippery and tiring to hold on to for long periods, especially if your horse is the forward-going type. You might consider reins with rubber grips or stops. Try them out with the gloves you intend to wear. We don't ride without gloves, even in hot weather: your grip and 'feel' are much better, as well as protecting your skin.

Headcollar or halter and rope

The most traditional method is to use a simple leather bridle over a halter or headcollar: it's easy to snap on a rope to lead the horse, or slip off the bridle at grazing time.

Rider's Tip – Saving your Reins

If you're leading the horse from a headcollar with the bridle still on, twist the reins round each other under your horse's jaw and feed one rein through the throatlash of the bridle for safety. It stops the horse treading on the reins or getting them caught round a gatepost. For very short stops, we use a home made nylon webbing and velcro loop attached to the saddle (see photo on page 129) – also handy when you need both hands free while mounted, perhaps to unfold a map. This stops the reins sliding down round his ears should your horse suddenly put his head down.

Breastplates

One of the principal differences between riding in an arena and out in the countryside is that you will almost certainly have to cope with some steep slopes. These can cause saddles to slip, especially on rounder, low-withered horses, or 'herring-gutted' animals, where the stomach slopes sharply upwards behind the girth.

If your saddle has a tendency to slip backward, a breastplate will be a useful addition to your tack, but it must be correctly fitted. It's not unusual to see horses with breastplates which are pressing on their windpipes, or interfering with the movement of horses' shoulders (or fitted so loosely that they might as well not be there!) The rule of the fist is a good one to remember when fitting a breastplate. In every area you should be able to fit your fist in with pinky next to the skin and thumb to the leather.

 See photographs on page 129 for examples of well-fitting breastplates.

Cruppers

Although we are perhaps more used to seeing cruppers on rotund Shetland ponies, or on driving horses, they can be a useful tool for the off-road rider too. They will help with a saddle which tends to slip forward going downhill, and are essential on a packhorse.

A horse wearing a crupper is at risk of becoming sore, unless it is correctly fitted. The most common error is to put it on too tightly: it should only come into play once the saddle starts to move forwards going down a steep hill. They will also (to a degree) help stop the saddle if it starts to shift sideways.

It should be fastened so that you can easily place a fist on the horse's rump, underneath the strap. The part which goes underneath the horse's tail must be smooth - traditionally they are stuffed with linseed. Care should be taken that it is kept clean - dried dung will make a horse sore very quickly. Some horses prefer the crupper lined with a sheepskin sleeve under the tail. Make sure the tail hair is lying flat and smooth.

Most horses adapt to them easily, but naturally you should try it out in a safe enclosed area, loosely fitted to begin with. It takes some horses a little while to become accustomed to the feel of something under the tail (and you may not want to be sitting on him while he's working it out.)

Saddlebags

Tempting though it may be to use a daysack or rucksack for your gear, you will find that they unbalance you, as well as making mounting and dismounting difficult. The range of saddlebags available has expanded considerably over the last few years to the point of being bewildering, although you are still likely to have to source them on the internet or by mail order, rather than at your local tack shop.

Good saddlebags...

Are robust and waterproof;

Are made of rip-proof materials;

Don't rub or irritate your horse;

Have strong fastenings that you can open/close with gloves on;

Are easy to locate items in quickly.

Countries such as the United States, which have a long tradition of trail riding, offer a greater choice than is currently available in Britain.

The cheaper saddlebags offered by discount stores may do the job in the short term (if it's not too wet!) but have a horrible tendency to split without warning. They generally offer very little in the way of padding to protect your horse and your camera, too. You can buy rigid-bodied cases in outdoor shops which will protect your camera or mobile phone from damp or impact.

A good material for saddlebags is heavy-duty ripstop nylon (similar to that used in good-quality outdoor rugs) with chunky fastenings. However careful you are, your saddlebags *will* get wet, rubbed, caught on a gatepost nail or dropped in the mud - the more robust they are, the better.

Good saddlebags are unfortunately not cheap. Looked after, they will last a long time though, so are worth the added expense. Some riders like leather saddlebags for durability (although they do take more looking after) but they can be heavy.

They are not too difficult to make if you're handy with a needle - remember to reinforce the seams though, as heavier items have the potential to rub through weaker seams when you're riding. See below for how to make serviceable saddlebags from recycled materials!

Ideally you want those heavier items in your front saddlebags, with lighter, bulkier items (like your waterproofs and spare fleece) behind the saddle. Packed saddlebags must weigh the same on both sides. You may want to put items in separate dry-bags (inexpensive and available in outdoor and camping shops). These offer additional protection from weather or tricky water crossings, as well as protecting items from burst or leaking bottles of liquid inside the packs. They are available in different colours, which makes locating items easier.

Your saddlebags, like all your equipment, will benefit from good care. This means emptying them immediately after every trip (forgotten mouldy sandwiches are not good for them, will rot the stitching and will encourage rodents to investigate); scrubbed and air dried, and re-proofed regularly, either with a spray, or wash-in reproofer.

An additional piece of equipment worth considering is a bumbag for yourself. In this you can carry items which you may need to get to quickly, as well as items you may need should you become separated from your horse: first-aid essentials, any personal medication, a snack, and your mobile phone.

What to put where is covered on the Day Ride Ticklist at the end of this chapter. For equipment for longer journeys, see Chapter 10 *Further and Higher, including Camping.*

To make serviceable saddlebags

These are not difficult to make if you – or someone you know – can sew in a straight line and have access to a sewing machine. The advantage of making them yourself is that you can alter the basic pattern to suit your own requirements.

These saddlebags can be used in front of or behind the saddle and include a padded, separate base pad. This does away with the need for extra large saddle pads. Because the base pad is detachable, it can be easily washed without having to put the whole caboodle through the washing machine.

There are adjustable Velcro straps to fasten the saddlebags to D rings at the front or rear of the saddle, and straps which fasten them to the girth straps on either side. All these fastenings ensure that the saddlebags will stay in place even at trot and canter, remaining comfortable for the horse and keeping your possessions safe.

If you are a more experienced sewer, you can customise the bags to meet your own particular requirements, adding additional padded pockets for your camera or other valuables.

Best of all, they are made from recycled materials: we used an old heavy duty waterproof horse rug for the saddlebags and an old quilted numnah for the base pad.

Making Saddlebags

Before you begin...

All seams are double–stitched for strength. You should use a machine needle designed for working with thick material – those sold for sewing denim are ideal.
All seam allowances are ¼".

What you need:

Quilted padded material for base pad (an old numnah is ideal);
Heavy duty ripstop nylon – about 2 metres x 40 cm for saddlebags and 2 metres x 15cm for gussets. We have used sections of an old waterproof outdoor horse rug, damaged beyond economic repair;
Suitable thread, such as a heavy duty polycotton;
2 pieces of wide elastic (for attaching saddlebags to the protective pad) each 40 cm long
Optional Two clips (for fastening to the D rings on the front or rear of the saddle.) These should be robust and easy to clip/unclip with gloved fingers. Tip: Check that they will go through the D rings *before* you sew them on.
3 metres of wide nylon webbing – for strengthening the back of the saddlebags, binding the edges and for making the adjustable girth straps.
3 metres of wide heavy duty velcro

Scissors
Chalk or tailor's chalk for marking up
Tape measure
Pins
Brown parcel paper or similar for making pattern.

Cutting and Marking

The pattern consist of five pieces: 1 x back piece; 2 x saddlebag fronts and 2 x gussets.

Step 1

Back piece.

Make up a paper pattern (A) according to the measurements in the diagram. (Note that line 1-2 is more curved than line 3-4 – this is so the finished saddlebags will fit easily around your saddle.) Mark the zig zag line (4 - 1) and the double dotted line (5-6) on your pattern. Round off bottom corners as shown.

Fold fabric, wrong sides together. Pin paper pattern (A) to the fabric, with the top of the pattern on the fold. Cut out. Mark the centre line 2-3 (of the fabric fold) with chalk. This is the back piece of your saddlebags.

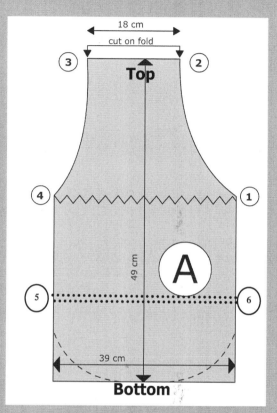

Step 2

Gusset. Make up a paper pattern (B) for the gusset. (This will form the sides and bottom of your saddlebags). Pin pattern to fabric and cut out 2 identical pieces – one for each bag.

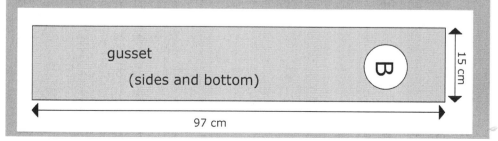

Step 3

Saddlebag fronts. Take pattern piece (A) and fold down at zig zag line 1-4. Cut out 2 pieces (zig zag line to bottom - these will form the front of the saddlebags). The fronts are exactly the same size as pattern piece (A) but only to the zig zag line.

Turn over 5mm hem to wrong side along top edge only, pin and stitch.

Step 4

Top piece and saddlebag flaps.

Take pattern piece (A) again, and this time fold up the bottom section at double dotted line 5 - 6. (You don't need the part below the double dotted line now).

Refold your material, this time with right sides together. Pin pattern piece (A) to the fabric with the top on the fold of the fabric. Cut out. Mark fabric fold centre line with chalk.

Pinning and Sewing

Step 5

Gussets.

Turn over 5mm hem to wrong side at both ends, pin and stitch in place. Pin gusset strip to front piece, right sides together, carefully easing material around corners. Stitch gusset in place using a double seam (this will give your bags much more durability). Clip the seams of any excess material, being careful not to clip through the stitching. Notch the corners.

Repeat for second saddlebag.

Step 6

Back piece. Nylon webbing attached to the back piece of the saddlebags will strengthen your bags. Pin two parallel strips of broad nylon webbing to the right side of the back piece and stitch.

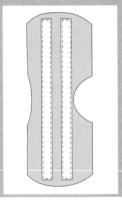

Step 7

Pin saddle bags to back piece, right sides together, easing excess material around corners. Stitch with a double seam. Clip excess material from seams, notching corners as in Step 4. Turn bags the right way out.

Step 8

Top piece and saddlebag flaps.

These will be more durable if the edges are bound with nylon binding. Bind the edges of the flaps first.
Place the top piece on top of the bags, aligning the chalk lines on back piece and top piece.
From the centre line, measure 13 cm on both sides.

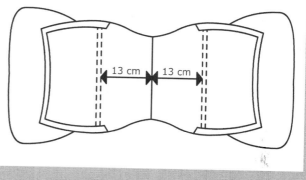

At the 13 cm mark, pin and stitch a double line of stitching. These rows of stitching attach the top piece to the saddlebags, and form the top of the flaps.

Step 9

Pin and stitch the remaining raw edges (the part which goes over the horse's withers or back) and bind with nylon binding.

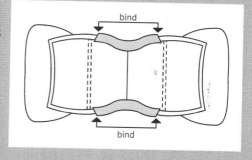

Step 10

Attaching the closures to the flaps.

We have used heavy-duty velcro, but you could if you prefer use buckles or snap toggles (of the type commonly used on rucksacks).
Cut the velcro to the length of the underside of the flap - check your own measurements, but it will be in the region of 37 cm.
Attach one side of the velcro to the underside of the flap, close to the bottom. Attach the other side to the front of the saddlebag, making sure both sides match up.

The velcro will need to be stitched in place - don't rely on the adhesive kind!

Step 11

Make your pad. Place the numnah on an ironing board, saddle horse or similar. Place the saddlebags on top.
Carefully draw around the bindings of the saddlebags with chalk, making the pad approximately 1 cm larger all round than the saddlebags.
Cut carefully along this chalk line. You will be left with some raw edges on the pad - sew these with a close zig zag stitch on your machine.

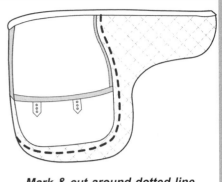

Mark & cut around dotted line

Step 12

Attach velcro to back of saddlebags and pad. A velcro strip is used to fasten the back of the saddlebags to the protective pad - about 6 cm from the bottom of the pad and the width of the back of the saddlebags is right. This stops the saddlebags flapping about on top of the pad, especially at trot and canter.

Step 13

Attach saddle fastenings to pad. You will need to attach two fastenings on each side: one to go through the D rings of the saddle, and one lower down to fasten around the girth straps. It's a good idea to try the saddlebags on your horse (tacked up) at this point, so you can mark the best place for these for your particular saddle. The side of the saddlebags with the *shallower* curve is the side you want next to the saddle.

Mark the four fixing points with chalk on the protective pad. Sew D rings to these points (we recommend taking the bags off the horse first!) You can use nylon straps with velcro attached to feed through the D rings on the pad and those on the saddle, or nylon or leather adjustable straps - whatever you have handy.

Step 14

Add elasticated loops to fasten protective pad to saddlebags. Stitch a strip of broad elastic (from point a to point b in diagram), just above the double seam which marks the saddlebag flaps. Repeat on other side.
These loops will help hold everything steady and together once you are actually moving.

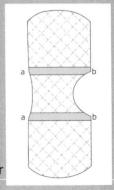

Step 15

Extra waterproofing. Your completed saddlebags will benefit from being treated with a waterproofing agent - either a spray or the wash-in kind.

Rider Clothing

Appropriate clothing, suitable for a range of conditions, is essential. It doesn't mean that you have to go out and spend hundreds of pounds on top of the range equipment (whatever the manufacturers of outdoor gear might tell you) - but you do need to approach it with some thought. Comfort and practicality should be your watchwords - not necessarily glamour! Waterproofs are a must, and you can get inexpensive but adequate jackets and trousers which pack down small for carrying.

You need to try and keep dry where possible. Wet clothing will rob heat from your body very much faster than dry clothing - that includes sweating. Wet clothing, as well as detracting from your enjoyment, also increases the risk of hypothermia in damp cool conditions (you'll meet plenty of them.)

In general, layers are a good idea, so that you can regulate what you're wearing for maximum comfort. You have the choice between natural fibres such as silk and wool which help keep you cool in summer and warm in winter, or garments made from newer synthetic fabrics which are designed to wick away moisture from your body (and generally dry quickly.) Cotton should be avoided (that includes jeans) as once it's wet, it never dries on you and you can end up thoroughly chilled. An extra fleece should always be carried: you never know when the weather might change, or you start to feel cold through illness or injury.

Whatever you choose, examine your garments carefully for seams which may rub when you're riding for hours - at best uncomfortable, at worst, exceedingly painful.

Particular attention should be paid to your feet and hands and a pair of dry socks in your saddlebags is a good idea, for when you've stepped in a stream or boggy ground. Even if your boots have got wet inside, dry socks will still make you much more comfortable. Cold wet feet or hands are guaranteed to detract from your enjoyment of the views. Some people find a silk liner sock with a heavier sock on top will help you avoid blisters, should you have to do a lot of walking off the horse.

Boots and Chaps

Caged stirrups, as described above, will increase your range of options. Many traditional riding boots are not comfortable to walk in for any length of time (as well as sometimes having poor grip in slippery conditions). A better choice is either a robust riding boot with a heel, or reasonably lightweight walking boots. Try and avoid anything too heavy in case you end up doing more walking than you expected. An old hillwalker's axiom worth remembering is 'a pound on the feet equals four on the back'!

From bitter experience, we can tell you that you are much more likely to get accidentally trodden on by your horse than you would be at home, as you negotiate muddy gateways or other tricky places, and your boots should be robust enough to protect you.

41

Many riders like wearing half or full chaps - these will also offer a measure of protection from branches and narrow gates.

Gloves

As mentioned elsewhere, decent gloves are a must - not only to keep your hands warm, but to protect them. If you're not the sort of person who loses things easily, a pair of top quality gloves designed for riding in all weather conditions (such as those worn by National Hunt jockeys) will prove a good investment. Otherwise, a spare pair of cheaper gloves should have a place in your saddlebags.

Gloves are a highly personal matter - what one rider adores another will hate, so try on plenty. Make sure that you are able to adjust tack, open saddlebags etc with them on, as well as being comfortable for holding the reins.

Other items

Other items worth carrying are a bandana or light balaclava (such as those made for made for motorcyclists) which you can put on under your helmet - you will have reason to be thankful when you crest a hill to get the full force of a freezing wind in your face. They are very light and pack down small.

It IS worth investing in good 'wicking' underwear which will help keep your skin dry. If you decide to buy some good underwear, such as that designed for walkers and climbers, bear in mind that they often have a definite ʹinsideʹ and ʹoutsideʹ. There are a number of internet sites which independently test outdoor gear - see Chapter **11** *Further Resources* for suggestions.

Day Ride Essentials

Headcollar (on horse under bridle) and long leadrope – 10 feet is good. Name and phone no on tag on headcollar, should the worst happen and you become separated from the horse;

Hi viz waistcoat and hatband (even if you're not planning on riding on the road.) It makes you easier to spot if you get lost; helicopters flying overhead will often take evasive action if they can see you early enough; and should you have to do a section of road for some reason, you are prepared.

Gloves & riding helmet (conforming to standard PAS 015 or EN 1384)

In bumbag:

Wire cutters (can also double up for removing a shoe). Note: these are not for gaily dismantling any fence you may come across, but in case your horse gets trapped in wire.

Penknife

Small first aid kit: Antiseptic cream (same for horse and human); Sterile wound dressing; Vetwrap or similar bandage; Triangular bandage; Paracetamol or other painkiller; space blanket; glucose tablets

Mobile phone (might not work everywhere of course). Better carried on you than on the horse as he may find it difficult to use in an emergency!

Whistle (the internationally recognised emergency signal is 6 blasts of the whistle (or 6 flashes of light from your torch) repeated at one-minute intervals.

In saddlebags

Waterproof jacket and trousers

Extra fleece or similar

Change of socks (so you had to lead him through the first ford and that's ok – but dry feet are more comfortable for the rest of the day)

Insect repellent

Sun cream (you can hope)

Camera

Lunch/snacks

Small torch (we carry one of the small wind-up ones, so no battery worries). We know you're not going to be out after dark, but...

Electrical tape or duct tape – for emergency repairs to your saddlebags or tack, or holding a dressing in place. You don't need a whole roll – a mostly-used one or some tape wound round a film canister is great.

Strong string – for tying up your horse

Antiseptic hand wash gel

Water bottle (plastic) – you can buy these to clip onto the saddle

Horse boot or boots You may wish to carry these in case of shoe loss or if you ride your horse barefoot but he needs more protection on flinty going.

Map and compass – we favour carrying these in clear plastic holders which you can wear on you for easy map checks. If buying one, look for a strong durable one – some are very flimsy. Alternatively, you can carry the map in a plastic bag in your bumbag.

Equipment

- should fit both you and your horse well

- should be robust and well-maintained

- is often a case of trial and error to find what suits you best - don't be afraid to experiment

- should be tested out on short rides at home first - don't wait until you're miles from home to discover problems

Where to Ride 3

Where am I allowed to ride my horse?

This is definitely something which confuses many riders! Unless you are particularly lucky, you are almost certainly going to have to be prepared to do some research before setting off. To make it slightly more complicated, the situation varies in different parts of the country.

Most land in the UK is in private ownership, including most woodland, forestry and national parks. This means you cannot necessarily roam free wherever you choose, but there are endless opportunities for off-road riding, provided you know where to look and understand your legal rights and responsibilities.

This chapter aims to :

• summarise the current legal situation regarding access in England and Wales, and in Scotland;

• explain what your responsibilites are as a rider;

• suggest ways of finding suitable routes;

• give you suggestions of who to contact for further information;

• give you tips on approaching landowners where necessary.

Access Legislation in the UK

ENGLAND & WALES

In England and Wales, the main basis for off-road countryside access is the rights of way system, which distinguishes between **footpaths** which are legally restricted to pedestrian access, and **bridleways**, which are open to horse-riders as well as walkers and cyclists.

Bridleways are shown on Ordnance Survey Landranger maps as long, dashed red lines, and on OS Explorer maps as long, dashed green lines. A public bridleway is sometimes waymarked using a blue arrow on a metal or plastic disc or by blue paint dots on posts and trees.

Bridleways may not always go in the direction you want to go, or provide the most direct route, but most of the time you can be relatively confident that if you follow the line on the map, you should be able to get through with a horse.

Other categories of route such as Roads Used as Public Paths (RUPPs) and byways are also usually accessible on horseback, and are also marked on OS maps.

A **permissive path**, or permitted path, is a path (which could be for walkers, riders, cyclists, or any combination) whose use by the public is allowed by the landowner, but over which there is no right of access.

A permissive path is often closed on a specified calendar day each year, and is usually clearly signed as a permissive path. These are precautions to prevent any possible future claim of continuous public access along the path, which could result in it becoming designated as a statutory right of way.

Permissive bridleways are shown as dashed orange lines on the 1:25,000 maps where there is no statutory right of way but where the landowner permits use, for the time being, as a bridleway.

Some farmers permit riding across their land by prior agreement or under licence. Your local authority may be able to give you the addresses of any toll-ride organisers or where paths have been created under Countryside Stewardship schemes and provide safe, off-road routes.

Did You Know?

By law, you are allowed to ride on bridleways, RUPPs/restricted byways and byways open to all traffic(BOATs). In addition, you can ride on what are quaintly termed carriageways, permissive bridleways and toll bridleways.

In England, some 37,000 km of rights of way (23% of the total) are known to be legally available for horseriding; In Wales, there are some 7,700 km (20% of the total).

In practice, many authorities and police forces would tacitly prefer that you rode on a footpath than alongside the busy main road nearby risking a horrible accident, but be aware you have no right to do this. If there is no alternative, you could try leading your horse, giving way politely to walkers (and clearing up any poo) and be prepared to be toe-curlingly apologetic to those you meet! (Better than being mangled by a lorry, let's face it.) If you have the landowner's permission, there is usually not a problem, provided you don't do any damage.

Bear in mind:

All bridleways should be passable but there is no guarantee as to the quality of gates, bridges or drainage conditions, nor whether they will be signed or waymarked. Infrequently-used tracks may be overgrown with vegetation.

On open ground the line shown on the map may not be evident on the ground. It is worth carrying a compass (and knowing how to use it.)

Very occasionally the line or status of a right of way may have been legally modified and is no longer exactly as shown on the map.

On high, exposed and on badly drained ground, many bridleways and tracks become impassable in wet weather and during the winter months.

By looking at your Ordnance Survey map, you can plan your route using bridleways and other legally-permitted tracks on the Public Rights of Way network. Note that areas defined on maps as 'access land' do not automatically provide open access for horse riding.

There are a range of statutory duties regarding public rights of way that are delivered by Countryside Access Teams across England and Wales, including:

- Asserting and protecting the public's right to use public rights of way;
- Maintaining public rights of way in a condition adequate to allow public use throughout the year;
- Keeping the definitive maps, which record all the registered public rights of way;
- Ensuring that landowners comply with the law, and do not interfere with the public right of passage;
- Signposting public rights of way where they meet a public road.

The Countryside Code

(England and Wales)

Code for the public

There are five sections of The Countryside Code dedicated to helping members of the public respect, protect and enjoy the countryside.

Be safe, plan ahead and follow any signs
Leave gates and property as you find them
Protect plants and animals and take your litter home
Keep dogs under close control
Consider other people

Code for land managers

There are three sections of the Countryside Code dedicated to land managers.

Know your rights, responsibilities and liabilities
Make it easy for visitors to act responsibly
Identify possible threats to visitors' safety

www.naturalengland.org.uk

ACCESS LEGISLATION — SCOTLAND

In Scotland since 2005 horse riders have benefited under the Land Reform (Scotland) Act 2003, which gives riders the same statutory right of responsible access as walkers and cyclists. It states the *rights* and *responsibilities* of those exercising access rights, as well as those of land managers and recreation managers.

As a rider, you have the right to access most land including mountains, moorland, woods and forests, grassland, fields, rivers and lochs, coastal areas, most parks and open spaces, golf courses (to cross them on established tracks); day and night, providing you do so responsibly. It also requires local authorities to uphold access rights.

The following guidance has been published jointly by The Scottish Rural Property & Business Association (www.srpba.com) and British Horse Society Scotland (www.bhsscotland.org.uk). The full guidance is downloadable on both of these websites and is well worth reading (even if you ride in England or Wales), as it clarifies what is meant by 'responsible access'. The guidance is designed to:

- foster mutual understanding and respect between horse riders, carriage drivers and land managers;
- clarify the legal basis for equestrian access in Scotland;
- suggest sources of further help and advice;
- identify how conflict can be avoided, or where necessary resolved.

Other relevant publications produced by BHSS include:

o **Are You Riding Responsibly? Equestrian Access Factsheets**

o **Horseriding and Carriage Driving on Scotland's Towpaths**

o **Outdoor Access and Dung Guidance**

All of these are available online at www.bhsscotland.org.uk/Pages/access.html, or hard copies are available on request from BHSS.

EQUESTRIAN ACCESS IN SCOTLAND

Who do rights of equestrian access apply to under the Land Reform Act?

- Individual horse riders and carriage drivers
- Groups of individuals riding or carriage driving together
- Some types of commercial activity such as pony trekking provided they are exercising their access rights responsibly.

Neither horse riders or carriage drivers, or any other member of the public exercising their legal right of access, are obliged to seek prior permission or to consult with land owners and managers, unless they wish to access land for activities which are not included within the provisions of the Land Reform Act. Some horse riders or carriage drivers may choose to contact land owners/managers to determine what they might meet along the way, for example to check whether gates are wide enough, but there is no requirement to do so, other than for the rider or carriage driver's reassurance that they will definitely be able to get through.

Where do rights of responsible equestrian access apply under the Land Reform Act?

- most paths and tracks
- open countryside – hills, mountains, moorland, grassland
- land in which crops have not been sown, including stubble
- margins of fields where crops are growing or have been sown
- grass fields provided they are not hay or silage fields at a late stage of growth
- woodland, forestry and policy plantings
- riverbanks, loch shores, beaches and the coast
  provided people act responsibly and follow the guidance in the Scottish Outdoor Access Code

Equestrian activities which are NOT included in the rights of access to other people's land:

- repetitive schooling
- use of facilities such as custom made gallops or cross country jumps
- building structures such as jumps or obstacles
- hunting
- rallies, competitions, other formally organised events
- vehicular access to such events or activities
- parking of lorries, trailers or other vehicles associated with such events or activities

Anyone wishing to carry out any of these activities on land other than that which they manage should seek prior permission from the land owner/ manager.

www.bhsscotland.org.uk   *www.srpba.com*

The Scottish Outdoor Access Code gives detailed guidance on your responsibilities when exercising access rights. The Land Reform Act sets out *where* and *when* access rights apply. The Code defines *how* access rights should be exercised.

The 3 key principles :

Respect the interests of other people:

Be considerate, respect privacy and livelihoods, and the needs of those enjoying the outdoors.

Care for the environment:

Look after the places you visit and enjoy. Care for wildlife and historic sites.

Take responsibility for your own actions:

The outdoors cannot be made risk–free for people exercising access rights; land managers should act with care for people's safety.

KNOW THE CODE BEFORE YOU GO

SCOTTISH OUTDOOR ACCESS CODE outdooraccess-scotland.com

The right of access does not of course mean that everywhere is suitable for riding – there may well be kissing gates or stiles en route to block your progress, or the going might not be suitable for horses. It's generally possible to find out though – see Making Further Enquiries later in this chapter. If you need to contact the landowner, you can also be sure you're not disrupting estate or farm activities, and you can arrange for horsebox parking and to get any gates unlocked (if required) at the same time.

Be a Responsible Rider!

We have a legal right to access many places but it's good practice to put yourself in the shoes of the landowner and imagine how you would feel if it was *your* driveway or field that someone was passing through on their horse. In a nutshell, this means:

- **not causing any damage**
- **not interfering with land managers'activities**
- **not interfering with or detracting from others' enjoyment of the countryside.**

By being thoughtful, it makes it more pleasant for people you meet as well as making it easy for riders to be able to pass through without fuss in the future. No–one would blame a landowner for losing the plot because a rider cantered past his cattle causing them to run blindly into a fence, bringing vet's bills and extensive repairs to the fencing.

NOT CAUSING ANY DAMAGE

- **Where possible, ride on firm or hard surfaces such as wide paths and tracks.**

- **Fields with crops in them should be avoided. If there is a right of access through them then stick to the path and do not be tempted to venture off it.**

- **Take extra care to prevent damaging fragile natural habitats and to avoid disturbing more sensitive birds and animals, particularly during the breeding season of April to July.**

- **Look after the places you visit and routes you enjoy: take only memories, leave only hoofprints.**

NOT INTERFERING WITH LAND MANAGERS' ACTIVITIES

- **Jumping walls and fences unnecessarily can be very irritating to land owners. If your horse knocks a stone this can lead to further damage to the wall – rather like a stitch coming loose can quickly cause the whole garment to fall to pieces! It can also be dangerous as it may not have a good landing or have hidden wires. So just because you think it CAN be jumped doesn't mean that it SHOULD be jumped.**

- **The same applies to stubble fields. Just because you can gallop round them it doesn't mean that you should. Apart from it being fairly unnecessary it leads to the kind of snorting horse that becomes unruly every time it goes into a stubble field: a bad habit which is entirely human created.**

- **Gates should always be left the way you find them. It's a good idea to carry some strong string with you so that you can always leave them stockproof – gates have a habit of collapsing sometimes. Don't assume all gates should be closed – they may have been left open on purpose to allow stock access to water.**

NOT INTERFERING WITH LAND MANAGERS' ACTIVITIES (cont)

•   If you see livestock in trouble, injured or stuck in a fence, then report this to the nearest house or farm. Don't assume that someone else will do this – they may have been checked already that day.

•   When passing livestock or other horses, don't stop to let your horse 'speak' to them as this can cause pawing forelegs or flying hindlegs – bad for fences and animals. Neither should you pass at speed: if sheep, cattle or horses see another animal travelling fast they generally assume that there is some danger. They may run also, causing damage to themselves and causing your own horse to get very upset. Pass purposefully at a walk.

•   Be prepared to adjust your route and/or pace to enable farm or estate activities to go ahead unhindered.

•   Respect reasonable requests to avoid certain areas to avoid potentially dangerous activities such as shooting, stalking, or timber felling.

•   Be considerate when parking: do not block tracks or obstruct entrances to fields or buildings.

NOT INTERFERING WITH OR DETRACTING FROM OTHERS' ENJOYMENT OF THE COUNTRYSIDE.

•   When passing other path users remember that a lot of people are unused to horses or may be scared of them. Try to stand to the side if you can or direct them to a safer place so that you can pass them safely.

•   If you are riding on a path used by walkers and cyclists and your horse passes droppings, dismount and kick them to the side. Although *we* know that it's not too offensive imagine the poor mum pushing her pram through it!

•   If you meet other horse riders, don't get too close or let the horses sniff each other. A kick can happen very quickly and take the best of us by surprise. It's polite to ask if they will be ok as you pass and head out of sight–they may be on a young horse who doesn't understand that they don't *need* to be with your horse! Again a purposeful walk is the best speed to cause the least upset.

•   A pleasant word with people you meet will make you (or other riders) more welcome the next time.

•   Always travel at a speed where you are under control and able to stop quickly. Remember no–one has checked that the ground is 100% safe and there could be a number of potential dangers to you and your horse, so it is YOUR RESPONSIBILITY to look ahead and be under good control.

The Landowner's View

Many off-road riders feel that the main issue causing problems with access isn't grumpy landowners, but the behaviour of a minority of other riders, which can cause problems for everybody. We're quite sure this doesn't apply to *you*, but the main causes of complaint from landowners include riders:

- allowing horses to dung inappropriately and not clearing it up (see page 64)
- travelling too fast or out of control
- disturbing farm animals or wildlife
- failing to shut gates
- jumping inappropriate obstacles or riding through growing crops
- parking horseboxes or trailers where they are an obstruction
- mucking out horseboxes & trailers at the side of a track
- behaving without courtesy to landowners or farmworkers they meet (ignoring them or being downright rude)
- being accompanied by dogs, over which they have inadequate control
- using paths or tracks when the ground conditions are extremely wet or otherwise unsuitable
- excessive noise, especially when riding in groups
- failing to take account of land management operations and making a nuisance of themselves.

Shooting (no, not *at* you)

One of the principal areas of potential conflict is during the shooting seasons. For many estates this is a major source of income, so they are understandably annoyed when these activities are disrupted by gormless riders wandering through. Shooting can take place on moorland (grouse, deer); woodland (pheasant, roe deer); arable (pheasant, partridge) and near wetlands (duck, goose).

This doesn't mean you can't ride across land during these seasons. What it does mean is that **you should obey signs and guidance from land managers and to stick to the agreed route.** This is for your safety (and that of your horse), as well as in the interests of good landowner relations and to avoid disturbing species. There is no shooting on Sundays.

In England and Wales, your rights of access on bridleways, RUPPs etc are unaffected: it's up to land managers to plan to avoid conflict with rights of way. In Scotland, land managers are required to use advisory signs, which should make it clear when the activities are taking place. The signs should be removed when the risk is over. Many Scottish estates also take part in the 'Hillphones' scheme during the deerstalking season which you can phone to get details of planned activities - details on www.snh.org.uk/hillphones. From 2010 they are also trialling a web-based service.

Be seen and be safe – hi-viz gear is a sensible precaution, particularly when riding through woodland. Riders may wish to check with the land manager, gamekeeper or estate office to find out when shooting is planned.

Main Shooting Seasons

Species	England, Wales & Scotland	
Pheasant	Oct 1 - Feb 1	
Partridge	Sep 1 - Feb 1	
Grouse	Aug 12 - Dec 10	
Hare	No closed season	
	Eng & Wales	**Scotland**
Red Stags	Aug 1st - Apr 30th	July 1st - Oct 20th
Red Hinds	Nov 1st - Mar 31st	Oct 21st - Feb 15th
Roe Bucks	Apr 1st - Oct 31st	Apr 1st - Oct 20th
Roe Does	Nov 1st - Mar 31st	Oct 21st - Mar 31st

Note: shooting of vermin can occur at any time. There is no closed season.

Planning Your First Rides

The purpose of these early rides is to build his confidence (and possibly yours). You want to finish the ride with a horse which is fit to continue, has not had a major fright, and has enjoyed his day. The distance you cover will probably be anywhere between 10 and 15 miles. To a car-travelling person, this doesn't sound like very far, but in the beginning this is ample and will give you both enough of a challenge. If your horse is young (or elderly), unfit, or if the route involves lots of hills, err on the cautious side. You may find that you have to walk with him for a proportion of the route if he tires more quickly than you expect– how fit are you?!

It's common sense, but with an inexperienced horse, we would try to avoid selecting routes with the following for our first few outings:

Road sections where heavy traffic may be expected;
Large sections of very soft or very stony ground;
Significant river crossings;
Steep hill sections (up or down);
Overgrown tracks where you have to push through dense undergrowth (can be the case in high summer or little–used tracks) if branches whipping against him are likely to worry him;
Difficult bridges (metal, narrow, without sides, suspension bridges);
Fields of frisky livestock.

In time he will cope with all these challenges (and many more) – but at the moment you are working on building his confidence. For these first few outings, keep it as simple and achievable for him as possible – there will be enough for him to think about without throwing in extra difficulties.

Day Rides

You basically have two options: to plan a circular ride, returning to your start point; or to plan a linear ride from point A to B (and arrange transport back). You might start from your home base (if you can do so safely without crossing major roads) or you might box to your start point.

Depending on your location, you might choose to ride a designated bridleway or horse trail or you might design your own routes using maps. Be aware that what looks like a good track on the map may not exist in reality, or may include locked gates, kissing gates or other non-horse-friendly hazards. If you are following a designated bridleway (in England and Wales) or a route promoted for horse riding (throughout the UK) your chances of getting stuck are naturally much less. There are some suggestions for finding horse-friendly routes near you in the sections Routes Promoted for Horse Riding and Who to Contact later in this chapter.

Overnight Stays

One option is to identify accommodation which you can use as a base for exploratory day-rides, returning to the same place each evening. These are often called 'petal rides': your accommodation is the centre of the 'flower', with each day's route forming one of the petals.

Many Horses Welcome and horse-friendly B & Bs are in locations which offer several different day rides from their base. A real advantage of this arrangement is that you don't have to lug all your gear (and your horse's) with you, or arrange for it to be transported, as you would if you were stopping at a different place each night.

On linear rides, where you are stopping at a different venue each night, you will have to transport your gear with you in saddlebags. If your horse needs rugs or lots of feeding, or you cannot live without several changes of clothing, you can arrange for your stuff to be moved for you by a co-operative friend or partner. Sometimes the B & B will do this, but expect to pay for this service.

Planning your route

Unless you are following a route mapped for you on a promoted route (and often, less formally, supplied by horse-friendly B & Bs, Horses Welcome hosts etc) you will need to do some planning. Access officers and rider access groups can be very helpful here, but note – they are NOT there to plan your riding holiday for you! What they will do is advise on local issues and conditions, and *may* be able to suggest accommodation for overnight stops, if you are clear about what you are wanting to do. But do your homework first:

- Roughly plan your route on the map. In England and Wales, life will be simpler if you stick to legally recognised horse routes such as bridleways. In Scotland, tracks marked with a double dotted line are generally much easier going than single dotted lines (although you may still have to make enquiries about locked gates).

- Once you have identified your route, you may wish to speak to an access officer (BHS or local authority) or local access group to check there are no obstructions. If you are in doubt about whether you have a right of access anywhere on your route, you can discuss this also. (Scotland only)

- In Scotland, you may wish to contact the landowner or his agent (see How to Find Out Who Owns the Land on page 63) to find out whether a track marked on the map is physically possible – bogs, collapsed bridges, and stiles are hazards best avoided on your early rides!

Rider's Tip – Searching for Information

Your search for places to ride will be made much easier if you have access to the internet (local libraries and community centres often have cheap or free access if you don't have access at home or work). The internet (at its best) allows frequent updating of information, but if you use it regularly you will know that this is not *always* the case...

Who To Contact (Further Information)

There are a number of organisations which you may find helpful in planning your ride – ranging from those which can advise on the legal position (including helping with access problems), to those which can help with routes or accommodation.

Rider Access Organisations

The British Horse Society (bhs.org.uk and bhsscotland.org.uk) offers advice and information about access and rights of way, as well as providing free leaflets on all aspects of riding. They also have a list of affiliated horse access organisations, as well as a national network of Access Officers.

The BHS also run the **Ride-UK** website (ride-uk.org.uk) and under construction at the time of writing) which aims eventually to give information on a national network of bridleways, including where you and your horse can stay overnight.

They are launching **EMAGIN®** (Equine Mapping and Geographical Information Network) in 2010. The project is a unique global equestrian database utilising digital Ordnance Survey maps of Britain and Ireland, displaying the National Bridleroute Network and all associated businesses at www.emagin.org.

Horses Welcome (horseswelcome.org) This is a bed and breakfast scheme for horses with quality assurance from the British Horse Society.

Other organisations

In addition, there are other organisations which can help with information and/or advice:

Equine Tourism (www.equinetourism.co.uk) offers information about horse holidays, accommodation providers with equestrian facilities

Geograph (geograph.org.uk) The Geograph project aims to collect geographically representative photographs and information for every square kilometre of Great Britain. While it doesn't offer routes, entering a grid reference will bring up multiple photos of the local area – very useful if you just want to see what a track, bridge or ford looks like while you're planning your route. Google Street View (maps.google.co.uk) can also be helpful in this regard, though only covering areas accessible by vehicle.

Sustrans (sustrans.org.uk) is the pioneer of the 'Safe Routes' concept in the UK – traffic free routes, including some very lengthy cycle routes across the country. Note that you can't automatically ride a horse along all of them (in some cases there are traffic barriers which prevent it) but they can provide some safe off-road alternatives, especially close to urban areas. Negotiations are ongoing to improve access for horse riders on these routes.

England & Wales

Byways & Bridleways Trust, The (bbtrust.org.uk) is a registered charity devoted to protecting Britain's network of ancient minor highways, which are generally referred to as 'byways and bridleways', and to expanding and adapting this network to take account of modern needs.

Countryside Council for Wales (www.ccw.gov.uk) champions the environment and landscapes of Wales as sources of natural and cultural riches, as a foundation for economic and social activity, and as a place for leisure and learning opportunities. Enter 'horseriding' into the search box for lots of information.

Department of Environment, Food and Rural Affairs (DEFRA) (www.cwr.defra.gov.uk) has a Conservation Walks and Rides Register with details of over 1600 walks and rides all over England and Wales. Some of these are quite short, but may prove invaluable in putting a route together.

Local Bridleways Society or Association There are very many of these: the best way to find one in the area in which you wish to ride is to search 'bridleways society' via your internet search engine.

National Federation of Bridleway Associations (www.rightsofway.org.uk)
The Federation provides a contact network to inform, support and encourage the many people and local groups working in isolation to improve bridleway access in their own areas.

National Trails (nationaltrail.co.uk) gives details of Britain's national long distance trails (currently 15). Sadly, they are not rideable end to end at the moment, but they all offer some long distance riding opportunities. At the time of writing, you can ride along the entire length of the South Downs Way and much of the Pennine Bridleway and along significant stretches of both the Ridgeway and Peddar's Way National Trails. Some other Trails have shorter lengths of bridleway so you should check on individual Trail pages on the website.

Natural England (naturalengland.org.uk) Informative website on countryside matters in England, including access. It has a selection of downloadable riding routes on its website.

Trails Trust, The (thetrailstrust.org.uk) is a charity that creates access to the countryside for all users including horse riders and carriage drivers. It is committed to creating multi-user paths and to ensuring that all cycle paths in England and Wales are available to all vulnerable non-motorised users, including horse riders.

Scotland

Heritage Paths (heritagepaths.co.uk) are aiming to collect as much knowledge of old paths in Scotland as possible and to promote the existence and the heritage of these paths. They have a searchable database with maps, including paths suitable for horses.

Old Roads of Scotland (oldroadsofscotland.com) This site aims to provide an overview of the history of roads and tracks in Scotland, particularly southern Scotland. Less for practical route planning than for finding out some fascinating information about Scotland's ancient byways.

Scottish Natural Heritage (snh.org.uk) is the principal body dealing with access in Scotland. You can download access legislation and the full Countryside Code here.In addition, their sister website **outdooraccess-scotland.com** offers advice and a comprehensive list of Scottish access contacts, including ranger services, local authority and national park access contacts and Scottish Natural Heritage access contacts.

Scottish Rights of Way Society (scotways.com) has been working to safeguard rights of way for 160 years. It is probably the oldest organisation in the world dedicated to improving countryside access. Their objects are the preservation, defence, restoration and acquisition of public rights of access for the public benefit over land in Scotland, including public rights of way. Although until recently primarily aimed at walkers, they are now considering the rights of other users too.

Major Landowners

This section deals with organisations that own or manage large parcels of land and who welcome horse rider access. They all have websites which give further information on access, including contact details.

National Parks (national parks.gov.uk) There are 15 National Parks in the UK and each one is looked after by its own National Park Authority. All of them welcome riders (not necessarily everywhere in the Park) and they can sometimes help with advice about overnight accommodation for you and your horse.

The Forestry Commission (forestry.gov.uk) is the largest land manager in Britain and the biggest provider of outdoor recreation. Generally they are horse-friendly and helpful, although be aware that due to ongoing forestry operations there may be areas you are not allowed to go. Forests are also sometimes used for other activities like car rallies or sled dog trials – each forest has a ranger who can advise about other planned events, any locked gates and about parking your horsebox. For contact numbers, see the website or the phone directory.

Horses are generally excluded from all-ability trails, designated footpaths and designated mountain bike tracks. The situation regarding access does vary from area to area: in Scotland there is pretty well access to all forested land (with the exceptions noted above): in England and Wales there is what is called a Concordat of Access, where access is encouraged although in some cases there is a charge.

The Ministry of Defence (mod.gov.uk)
The Defence Estate contains some of the most stunning landscapes in Great Britain. Its scenery, rich heritage and comparatively remote nature have created a valuable recreational facility that the public may use and enjoy. In addition to walkers, the estate is used by the public for horse riding, cycling and other recreational activities.
Many routes across rural sites are accessible to horse riders. The Ministry of Defence do point out military activities can be noisy or have the potential to startle, so rider safety is of paramount importance. They highlight some important safety advice for horse riders when visiting the estate on their website, where you can also download *Military Helicopter Low Flying Safety – A Guide for Riders.*

The National Trust (nationaltrust.org.uk) is one of Britain's largest landowners, owning or managing some 1% of the country (almost 600,000 acres.) Although not all of their properties are suitable for riding, the National Trust is sympathetic and supportive of horse access, where this is practicable. On some properties, a permit system is in operation.

The National Trust welcomes equestrian access on its land and seeks to promote and extend provision in conjunction with its farm tenants wherever appropriate. It tries to offer safe off-road routes, uphold public rights of way and contribute to a wider network on its own and neighbouring land.

The National Trust for Scotland (nts.org.uk) is the conservation charity that protects and promotes Scotland's natural and cultural heritage for present and future generations to enjoy. With over 310,000 members it is the largest conservation charity in Scotland. Like its English counterpart, it promotes access to the countryside generally, and horse riding is possible on many of the properties. Each countryside property has a ranger service who can advise on access.

The Crown Estate (thecrownestate.co.uk) includes agricultural estates of approximately267,000 acres and forestry estates of nearly 27,000 acres. They offer open access to almost 70,000 acres of land, in addition to some 800 kilometres (500 miles) of public footpaths and bridleways. Efforts are focused on the development of new permitted access routes in appropriate areas.

How to Find Out who Owns the Land (or Inspector Clouseau's Handy Hints for Off-Road Riders)

In an ideal off-road rider's world, we can just saddle up and go without having to seek 'permission'. In many places you can do just that: promoted riding routes, enlightened estates, official bridleways and many forests and national parks. But how do you *know* you're not going to come across a locked gate, a broken-down vehicle blocking the path, or an impassible bridge? Well, research before setting off will help of course, but sometimes, particularly if you're planning your own cross-country route, the simplest thing to do is to ring up the landowner (or his or her agent - who may be a keeper, a stalker, or tenant farmer.)

Why should I speak to the landowner/land manager?

By law, you don't have to speak to them at all (if you are following bridleways, routes promoted for riding or other horse tracks in England, or anywhere in Scotland where you have the right of responsible access.) However, it can be of benefit to you (and them):

- to check if there are land management/farming operations which may mean you need to divert your route or which may hold you up, including timber operations, moving livestock, quarry operations, maintenance of rivers and canals or moor burning
- to check local ground conditions, particularly after periods of heavy rain or flooding;
- to seek advice if you know you are going to have to ride through fields or open areas where there are livestock – cows with calves at foot can be *extremely* aggressive.
  You must speak to them:
- if you are going to require somewhere to park a horsebox – unless there is an area set aside for this purpose;
- if you wish to negotiate grazing for your horse(s) or to camp.

Contacting landowners (where appropriate) is courteous, responsible and makes riders more welcome in future.

How do I know who to contact?

There are a number of strategies which we have found helpful in locating the right person. As time goes on, you will develop your own network of contacts (all off-road riders have them) which will help you to get in touch with the right person quickly. In the meantime:

Phone directory Even if you don't know the name of the person, estates and large farms are often listed under their own names

Internet If you search the name of the estate, it will often lead you to a person's name (and telephone number, if you're lucky)

Access and Bridleway Officers (at the council, or the British Horse Society) can often be helpful in identifying who you need to speak to

Local Bridleway or Rider Access Groups are often helpful too, and are usually aware of track obstructions, mad farmers, etc

Other riders/horse people We have had great assistance, when riding in unfamiliar areas, from people in endurance and riding clubs and breed societies

Other landowners Naturally, they always know who their neighbours are (even if they're not currently speaking to them) so if you're in contact with one landowner, it's good policy to find out who you need to speak to next door.

National Park rangers have a list of contacts on their particular patch – and can advise on whether they feel it's appropriate to speak to the person or if it's fine just to ride through.

Poo Matters!

Compared with dog faeces, horse droppings offer little in the way of health hazards to humans. However, it is perhaps *the* major issue for other path users, who may find it offensive and a matter for complaint. While there is no legal requirement to do so, in the interests of harmony in the community, dismount and kick it to the side:

On any formally-surfaced path

On any path used by wheelchairs or walkers with prams or buggies

On cycle paths – hitting a pile at speed is definitely not funny

On towpaths

On driveways or access routes to a house

Routes promoted for horse riders

These can be a great place to start: you know that much of the work in finding passable routes has been done for you. In many cases, accommodation for you and your horse is easily available (although may be booked up well in advance in the summer).

The following is by no means an exhaustive list, but will give you some ideas to follow up. To source more information on these rides, we have given website addresses – also see *Who to Contact – Further Information* earlier in this chapter.

PROMOTED ROUTES (ENGLAND & WALES)

Various long distance routes have been developed in England and Wales - some specifically for horses. The physical quality of the routes varies as much as the location and length. Many of those described or developed in the past by local volunteers have never been formally waymarked, nor have they necessarily had any capital funding to upgrade to horse-friendly gates, but on the whole, you should be more confident of being able to ride promoted routes than other bridleways.

North England

- **Pennine Bridleway** (www.nationaltrail.co.uk/PennineBridleway) – 120 miles of this linear route up the spine of northern Britain has been opened so far, including the southern section from the bespoke faciliaties at the southern terminus at Hartington in Derbyshire through to the **Mary Towneley Loop**, north-east of Manchester, and the **Settle Loop** in North Yorkshire. The northern extension from Kirkby Stephen to Northumberland is still under development. The whole route has been developed to a high standard and detailed route and accommodation guides are available for the sections which have been opened.
- **Heritage Ride** (ride-uk.org.uk) 250 mile linear route through Lincolnshire, East and North Yorkshire (but you will need a trailer or box to get across the Humber Bridge) It crosses the Newtondale Trail.
- **Newtondale Trail, North Yorkshire** (www.northyorkmoors.org.uk) Circular 37.5 mile route of wonderful riding across the purple heather of the North Yorkshire Moors
- **Bishop Bennet Way** (discovercheshire.co.uk) 34 mile route in Cheshire. The website offers other riding options in this area.

Midlands

- **www.ridewelland.co.uk** – promoting equestrian tourism and riding routes around east Leicestershire and Rutland
- **Sabrina Way** (ride–uk.org.uk) linear route between the southern end of the Pennine Bridleway in Derbyshire and Gloucestershire, linking to the Jack Mytton Way in Shropshire/Worcestershire. Note: at the time of writing, some sections are overgrown with vegetation and most of the waymarkers have disappeared. Four separate leaflets describing the route should be available from BHS or the relevant county council access officers.
- **Jack Mytton Way** (shropshire.gov.uk) Originally a linear route through Worcestershire and the Welsh Borders, recently upgraded to include circular option(s), with horse and rider accommodation directly on route. Links up to the Prince Llewellyn Ride in the Welsh Borders.

Wales

- **Three Rivers Ride** – linear route from Hay Bluff to the visitor centre in the Brecon Beacons. http://www.horseridingbreconbeacons.com
- **Prince Llewellyn Ride** (ride–uk.org.uk) linear long distance ride across mid–Wales from Llanfair Waterdine, near Knighton, in the east all the way to the beach at Borth, near Aberystwyth. (You can devise your own circular route back to base using other bridleways). Leaflet available from BHS. Be aware that most of the route is not currently waymarked, is difficult to follow in places, there are some boggy sections and some of the sections identified on the leaflet as off–road are in fact on road, but spectacular scenery with horse and rider accommodation en route and a brilliant beach to gallop along once you hit the coast.
- **Seahorse Ride** – 53–mile linear long distance route in North Wales stretching from the northerly coast down to the A5 at Glyndyfrdwy.
- **William Morgan Ride** – linking the Seahorse and Prince Llewellyn Rides

Southern England

- **The Ridgeway** (ride–uk.org.uk) is one of the oldest routes in Britain, a fantastic linear route along the top of the downs, the western part of which is open to horses. It is not difficult to plan a circular route back to the start on other bridleways taking in Watership Down and other interesting places.

  The **Three Downs Link** passes through the chalk downland of Berkshire, Oxfordshire, Wiltshire and Hampshire, joining together the two National Trails of **The Ridgeway** and **The South Downs Way**.

PROMOTED ROUTES (SCOTLAND)

- **South of Scotland Countryside Trails** (southofscotlandcountrysidetrails.co.uk)
The South of Scotland is renowned for having some of the best horse riding
country in Britain and offers a 350km network of waymarked off-road routes.
Also includes:
Tyne Esk Trails. Sixty miles of horse trails comprising four circular routes, each
between 10 – 15 miles long. Explore a wide variety of glorious Midlothian

- **Galloway Forest Park** Dumfries & Galloway (www.forestry.gov.uk/scotland).
More than 650km of off-road riding. A leaflet showing the extent of the Park,
places to park horse boxes etc is   available from Forest Enterprise, Creebridge,
Newton Stewart DG8 6AJ. (SAE required.)

- **Buccleuch Country Ride** (www.bowhill.org/public/bowhillcountrypark/horseriding)
Scottish Borders 90km of horse-friendly trails with accommodation. Map of trails
published by Harvey Maps (www.harveymaps.co.uk)

- **Trail of the Seven Lochs** (www.southlochnessaccess.org.uk). 50-mile
loop route near Loch Ness on the Highlands providing stunning views and varied
terrain

- **Moray Equestrian Access Group** (www.meag.org.uk) for suggested routes in
and around Morayshire (North East Scotland).

- **BHS access groups** (bhsscotland.org.uk/Pages/access_groups) – at the time of
writing, there are fourteen affiliated access groups covering much of Scotland, who
can offer advice on routes in their area. Some include maps and route
descriptions on their websites.

- **Long distance paths** Most long distance routes were developed prior to the Land
Reform Act. The whole of the Great Glen Way and some sections of the Southern
Upland Way, West Highland Way and Speyside Way are rideable, but there are
many sections which are not suitable for horses because of the gradient, terrain
or deep peat, and/or where use is restricted by stiles, kissing gates or other similar
access controls impassable with horses. For further information on these routes,
check with the route manager.
Dava Way (www.davaway.org.uk)
Great Glen Way (www.greatglenway.com)
Southern Upland Way (www.southernuplandway.gov.uk)
Speyside Way (www.greatglenway.com)
West Highland Way (www.west-highland-way.co.uk)

- **Forestry Commission Scotland** (www.forestry.gov.uk/scotland) offer many off-road riding opportunities in Scotland, including the huge Galloway Forest Park in Dumfries and Galloway, Glenmore Forest Park near Aviemore and Queen Elizabeth Forest Park in the Trossachs.

- **Local Authority Core Path Network** Under the Land Reform Act, each local authority in Scotland has been required to identify a network of core paths in their area. Whilst not all are suitable for horse riders, many are, and most authorities have a map of the core paths on their website, as well as Access Officers who can advise.

What's a Core Path? (Scotland only)

Core paths were brought in under the Land Reform (Scotland) Act. The purpose of the core path network is to provide a framework of routes to give the public reasonable access throughout their area. They also often link into other paths and tracks which are not part of the core path network.

Core paths can be anything from a stony track across open ground to a specially-constructed path suitable for wheelchair users. It's important to recognise that not all are necessarily suitable for horses, and to be particularly diligent about the rights of other path users on shared paths, including removing dung, travelling at a safe speed, and passing pedestrians in a safe manner.

At the time of writing, not all Councils and National Parks have fully adopted their Core Path Plan, although many have and most of the others are a long way through the process. Many Councils publish their core path maps on their websites, or can provide you with a map, as well as advice about the suitability of a particular core path for horses.

Note that while a Council may have adopted a route as a core path, they do not necessarily have responsibility for maintaining it.

A complete list of Scottish local authorities can be found at
outdooraccess-scotland.com
For more information on core paths, see
bhsscotland.org.uk/Pages/core_paths.html

Got An Access Problem?

Sadly, it happens - somewhere where you thought you could ride turns out to be impassable. This could be for any number of reasons - locked gates, stiles, cycle barriers, barbed wire or electric fencing strung across tracks, or a landowner or householder who refuses to let you through.

Sometimes access problems are deliberate (a landowner refusing to allow riders through their land) and sometimes they are the result of someone just not considering the needs of horses (eg putting up gates to stop motorbikes will effectively stop horses too).

In England & Wales:

Either you have the right to legitimately ride on a track or path, or you haven't: the situation is reasonably clear cut. If you believe you have the right and someone or something is stopping you from exercising it, you will need to seek further advice:

- **The British Horse Society, who have a network of Access and Bridleways Officers**
- **Countryside Access Teams (each local authority has one and their contact details are generally accessible on the relevant local authority website))**

In Scotland:

Try contacting the landowner and explaining calmly and politely your proposed route. They may have legitimate objections (or not!) They may simply have not considered horse access - this has been our experience in many areas of Scotland, and usually a way round the problem can be found. Negotiation and compromise are good watchwords. If a landowner offers a compromise such as an alternative route, you should be prepared to consider this. Do not get into an argument, however frustrated you may feel.

If it's a track you would like to ride regularly, you may be able to offer support to the landowner in return for access, for example by roping in other riders to volunteer to clear an overgrown track or clear ditches to improve drainage. There are various methods of accessing funding to, for example, put in self-closing bridle gates, which may resolve a problem for the landowner (and you).

For more support and advice, contact:

- The British Horse Society Scotland
- Local rider access groups
- Local Authority Access Officers

Finally, please consider getting involved with access yourself: through the BHS (which is the only national body with an access remit, and therefore tends to be the one involved in consultations with politicians and other decision-makers regarding rider access), a local rider access group, a bridleways group or similar. Other people have given up their time to ensure we have places to ride, and you too can help.

Where to ride

- educate yourself on the legal position, taking account of the differences north and south of the border

- remember that in finding out where to ride, it's often necessary to do some prior research

- be a responsible rider, considerate towards land owners and other path users

- plan early rides with particular care, taking account of the needs of your horse and yourself

- consider exploring some of the many routes promoted for horse-riding

- consider getting involved with access yourself

The Training Starts Here

4

Manners Maketh Horse

Good manners both on the ground and under saddle are desirable in any horse, of course, but in the off-road horse they are extra important – your enjoyment, comfort and safety depend on it. Quite a few riders will accept less than mannerly behaviour from their horse, feeling it doesn't matter all that much if he won't stand still to be mounted or saddled, makes a beeline for the nearest patch of grass, turns his rump to them when they go to catch him or barges them out of the way when his feed arrives.

On a hillside, you don't have the luxury of a box to put him in (or sometimes nowhere to even tie him up) while you adjust his tack, pick out his feet, or fight with a gate.

Only you can decide what is acceptable behaviour to you, but how much more pleasant (and safer) to have a horse you can manoeuvre easily, who works willingly with you as part of a team, and who you can trust to behave himself in any circumstances.

Virtually every horse can be improved in his manners: the sheer amount of time you spend with him, providing you are *persistent* and *consistent* in your handling of him, will develop him into a horse who truly appears to respond to your very thoughts. The only possible exception is a horse who has been abused or traumatised in the past by a previous owner – these horses can also be helped, but you may need someone experienced with this type of animal to aid you, at least in the beginning.

In order to have a horse you can trust, you need to look at your own skills too - are you a trustworthy leader and partner for *him?*

The areas we are going to examine in this chapter are:

his manners on the ground
your horse awareness and handling

A number of different self assessments follow to help establish whether you need to do more homework before setting out. If you can tick them all then hopefully this will give you both the confidence to go out and give it a go! If not then we will take you through some exercises which will help you both.

Assessment One – Ground Manners

Does your horse:

- **stand still until you tell him to move?**

- **lead politely *from both sides*, without hanging back, barging off or treading on you?**

- **lead without resistance into the trailer, over bridges, through water?**

- **lift all four feet to be attended to without a battle?**

- **back up on command?**

- **move over?**

- **tie up quietly without fuss?**

- **respect your personal space?**

These are things that you should expect from your horse on a daily basis. They not only provide you with a horse that is easy to handle but also provide the basis of a good partnership. Be assured if he doesn't do them at home, he's not going to do them out on the trail, when he is excited or nervous!

WHY DOES MY HORSE NEED TO STAND STILL?

- You are out riding when you come to a dilapidated gate, tied up with barbed wire and baler twine. The ground around the gate is knee deep in mud, and you have to get off and bodily lift the sagging gate open. How much easier it is when your horse has been trained to stand still, leaving you with both hands free.

- On a twenty–mile ride, you find you have to dismount a dozen times for gates and to lead your horse over narrow bridges. Not a problem, because although you are starting to get a bit stiff, you know without a shadow of doubt that your horse will stand like a rock while you clamber back on from a gate or bank.

- One of the great pleasures of exploring the countryside is chatting to people you meet. Your horse will stand motionless until you pick up the reins to move off, without pawing, pulling on the reins, dancing sideways or fidgeting.

- You are riding past a field of young heifers who come barrelling towards your horse, snorting and bucking. Instead of whipping round and setting off for home, your horse responds to the command to stand. When you're ready, he walks on quietly.

- You're riding across a moorland track, miles from anywhere. The track was rougher than you had anticipated, and you hear a clanking which tells you a shoe is about to come off. You hop off and get your horse to stand while you get the shoe off and fit a boot.

TEACHING YOUR HORSE TO STAND

In order to teach him to stand, you need to practise **often**. Use every opportunity: out on a ride, when you're tacking up, or leading him in and out of the field. Apply common sense - don't ask for too much while he's learning if the local hunt is galloping past - eventually, you will train him to stand even then.

You need a consistent verbal command. We use two words to differentiate between halting from movement ('whoa') and standing still once he's halted ('stand'). "Whywontyoustandstillyouhorriblefatponyowthatsmyfootgetoff" may confuse him.

Practise asking him to stop using your word along with a physical pressure on the nosepiece of the headcollar which is released when he responds. Reward him with a release of pressure and a scratch on the neck.

Once he is halting successfully, you can then try moving yourself while making him stand still. Can you walk right round him? Away from him? (a couple of steps at first, then further away). To begin with, he may step towards you. Put him back where he was and repeat the exercise, praising him when he does as you ask.

He may be surprised - and even a bit bolshy - at your new-found determination that 'stand' really *means* 'stand'. Stick with it and be consistent - if you're sometimes firm and sometimes let him move about, you can't really blame him for trying it on, can you?

Try this!

You have to allow him to make mistakes, or he'll never learn...don't try and hold him still (it won't happen).

If you pay attention, you will spot the signs that he is *about* to move: his muscles will tighten and he may move his focus away from you.

At this moment (before he has actually taken a step) a low growl will often remind him what he's *supposed* to be doing.

Rider's Tip – Unwilling to Stop

If he's unwilling to halt or stand, you can try using an obstruction such as the side of the arena, a fence or a tree. Walk him towards the obstruction and when you meet it give the verbal and physical command.

WHY DOES HE NEED TO LEAD WELL?

- You are walking across a steep slope leading your horse from the nearside and he is on the upside of you. His feet are slipping down towards you and suddenly your 15hh cob seems like a 17hh Shire. Being able to lead from the off–side so that you are above him would be much safer.

- You are leading your horse along a very narrow path, where there is not room for both of you to walk side by side. The horse bashes in behind you, tries to push past you and clips your heels. Having him trained to lead behind you quietly would be safer and more pleasant.

- You are riding one horse and leading a packhorse. You have covered 5 miles and your back has a slight twist to the right, causing a twist in your seat as well as holding on to the reins constantly with just your left hand. This is making you tired as well as unbalancing the horse you are riding. The pack horse has also been carrying his head and neck slightly to the left. With all this imbalance it would be great if we could swap the side in which the pack horse was being led for the next 5 miles.

TEACHING YOUR HORSE TO LEAD

Good ridden work starts with good ground work. A horse who doesn't lead well is frankly unlikely to suddenly turn into an angel when you mount.

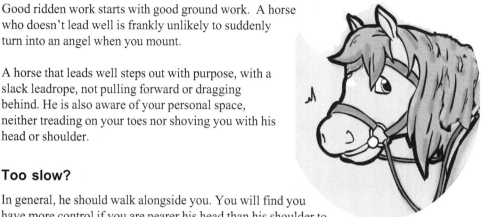

A horse that leads well steps out with purpose, with a slack leadrope, not pulling forward or dragging behind. He is also aware of your personal space, neither treading on your toes nor shoving you with his head or shoulder.

Too slow?

In general, he should walk alongside you. You will find you have more control if you are nearer his head than his shoulder to begin with. If he has a habit of lagging behind then carry a whip (with something nice and rattly like a plastic carrier bag tied onto it if he is extra lazy.) You don't need to smack him - just give him a "flick" behind you on his quarters every time he starts to drift back. When he steps out smartly, praise him. Make sure you're not constantly nagging him to keep up - he must be allowed to find out that if he doesn't step out, discomfort will follow. When he does as you ask, let him know that's what you want - he's not a mindreader!

You need to practise and you must be consistent - it's no good allowing him to drift along behind you in a daydream when you're bringing him in from the field, and then expect him to lead perfectly when you're out somewhere strange.

Too fast?

If he walks too fast, short, intermittent pulls on the nose-piece will stop the horse from leaning weight into the head-collar and pulling. Use your voice to steady him. Try stopping or changing direction every time the horse pulls to show him that *you* are in control of pace and direction. Again, it is very important to remember to praise him when he does well - it must be clear to him what is the right thing to do.

Once he's 'got it', you will be able to lead him anywhere, fast or slow, from either side through many changes of direction, over poles or past obstacles - and the lead rope will remain slack at all times, because he's working with you and watching your body language. Now that's something to aim for.

The halters used by 'natural horsemanship' trainers such as Pat Parelli, Kelly Marks or Richard Maxwell can be a very effective tool in training the headstrong horse, but they *must* be used intelligently and with care, and with full understanding of the principles of pressure and release. Some suggestions for further reading are given in Chapter **11** *Further Resources*.

Leading past obstacles

This is easily practised at home first: most horses will conveniently spook at unfamiliar objects on 'their' territory! Remember when you left the wheelbarrow upside down in a strange place?

One of the main reasons for spooking is that horses don't see the way we do; nor do they appear to logically work things out: "Oh that's the wheelbarrow I see every day – she must have dumped it there when she had to rush to the loo" is not really in their repertoire. There is no doubt that spooking can sometimes be a form of nonsense and disobedience, to get out of doing something, or just because he's feeling particularly well and full of beans. Whatever the reason, spooking can be very unseating if you're riding (especially if he also whips round), and dangerous to your wellbeing if you're leading him.

However, remember that if you practise the skills in this chapter you can manoeuvre him where you want him to be, and get him to stand in place, and these are key factors in managing spook behaviour.

In a fenced space such as an arena, place an unfamiliar object – a small tarpaulin draped over a chair is good, or a large exercise ball – something he's not used to. (Best not to try this exercise when other yard members are riding in the arena, by the way...)

Lead him into the arena and stand a good way away from the target. Let him look, reassure him, but encourage him to stand still while he examines this strange object. Once he is standing quietly, ask him to move forward a few steps, but not directly towards the object to begin with. Then ask him to move on again, then stop. If he is standing goggling at the object with his head held high, encourage him to lower his head to help him to relax.

Your object at this stage is to get him to proceed round the arena at a safe distance from the target, with you (the safe leader) between him and the object. Be firm, but don't force him up close to it too quickly.

*You want me to do **what**??*

Once he's leading quietly round the target in one direction, turn round and lead him the other way, again keeping yourself between him and the target. Be prepared for him to act as if he's never seen it before! The advantage of being between him and the scary thing are two-fold: one, you are showing him (again) that you are the safe leader, and two, should he suddenly jump sideways he will jump away from the object (and you) and not right on your foot.

You can gradually spiral in a little closer to the target, with lots of praise and reassurance. Extra praise is due if he eventually reaches out to touch it with his nose, but don't force it – it's not necessary. Out riding, you merely want him to pass things once you, the glorious leader, have reassured him that it is safe – he doesn't need to touch them.

Rider's Tip – Leading Your Horse

There is absolutely no disgrace in getting off to lead your horse past something (although you will meet people who say that it is – ignore them.) Putting yourself between the horse and the object is a good strategy which will give him confidence – and it does underline why it's important that he leads obediently from both sides.

When you're passing an obstacle, it helps if you don't look at it – focus beyond it, up the track, and your horse will too.

PICKING UP FEET

WHY DOES MY HORSE NEED TO PICK UP HIS FEET EASILY?

This is such an important discipline, as well as being an exercise in trust. It is also much easier for your farrier to do a first class job if he's not struggling to get your horse to hold a foot up. It's a good exercise to do combined with the standing still exercises, because there's often nowhere convenient to tie him up on a ride. As well as attending to his feet, this training will also make it easier for you to deal with any leg wounds, removing thorns from his legs and so on.

You will need to attend to your horse's feet on a long ride, whether that is picking out stones or fitting a boot because a shoe is cast. You definitely want your horse to lift up his feet politely, without snatching, leaning on you or trying to kick.

Picking up feet safely:

Tie your horse up before you begin while he's learning. Ultimately you will be able to do it on the side of an open hill, but to begin with, it's easier if he's standing still.

- Starting at the near fore, pat your horse on the shoulder.
- With your left shoulder at your horse's shoulder facing the rear of the horse, run your left hand down the back of the leg.
- As you get to the pastern slide your hand to the inside of the leg cupping the front of the pastern. Use the command 'up', add a little pressure with your elbow which will be at the back of the horse's knee and the horse should lift the foot.
- Use your right hand use the hoof pick.

For the near hind:

- Pat your horse's shoulder and run your hand to his hindquarters.
- With your left shoulder at your horse's hindquarters and facing the back run your left hand down to the hock.
- At the hock turn your hand to the front of the hind leg and run it down to the front of the pastern.
- At the pastern run your hand to the inside of the pastern and cup it, giving the command 'up'. Leaning into the back of the leg should encourage your horse to lift his leg.

If you lift the legs in this way you reduce the chance of your arm being broken should the horse suddenly kick out.
The procedure for picking up the off side feet is exactly the same, but reversed: i.e it will be your right hand patting and running down your horse's leg, not the left.

When you are comfortable picking up the feet in this routine then start to change the leg you pick up first. Your horse will not be so surprised when you pick up the random foot which has lost a shoe when you are out riding.

For a horse which is unwilling to pick up his feet, squeezing his chestnut (the horny growth on the inside of the leg) with your free hand will generally encourage him to smarten up his ideas quickly.

If you always tap his leg first and use a verbal cue like 'up', he will learn to lift his foot just from the tap – nice when those hooves are covered in mud.

The sequence of photographs on page 134 show how to pick up your horse's feet safely.

Rider's Tip – Picking Up Feet

Another trick is to be able to pick up all your horse's feet from one side. This is a carriage driving technique which allows the groom to pick out the horse's feet from the free side of the horse when he was part of a pair or a team. Thoroughbreds in racing stables are also generally taught to do this, for speed and efficiency.

The advantage for you is it means you can pick up any foot out on a ride where space is tight, for example on a narrow path.

How to do it

Make sure your horse is happy to pick up all his feet normally.

When you are on the near side of the horse having picked up the near fore and placed it down, reach over to the off fore and cup the pastern lifting it and bringing diagonally behind the near fore to pick it out. Don't forget to use your verbal command.

To do this with a hind leg you should again pick up the near hind, place it down then reach to the front of the off hind, cupping the fetlock and crossing it over in front of the near hind to pick it out. Please do not cross the hind leg behind the near hind as this increases the risk of you being injured if the horse decides to kick out. Practise doing this from both sides.

BACKING UP

A horse who backs up obligingly on command will make your expeditions much easier. For example:

- **he is easy to manoeuvre when you are trying to mount off a gate or a bank;**
- **you can use it to immediately avoid a bog, or a roll of wire you have spotted lying in the grass;**
- **it makes opening gates much easier;**
- **you can back up safely to a wider part of the path if you meet another track user where it's too narrow to pass;**
- **it's an excellent way of getting him to respect your personal space;**
- **you can use it to get him past an obstacle, when all else fails!**

We often ask the horse to go back without realising when walking into the stable or at the gate into the field. Become conscious of this and emphasise the manoeuvre.

Use the verbal command "Back" or Back up" whilst applying prodding pressure on his chest and perhaps the head-collar. Keep the pressure light at first, making it stronger if he doesn't respond. Don't lean against him with a steady pressure - he'll just lean back.

When he responds and takes a step back reward him by releasing the pressure and a small scratch, and praise him. Remember to use the same word each time - he'll remember this when you start teaching him to back up under saddle, and if you practice, eventually he will respond just to the word, without the prodding.

Ideally you want him to back up slowly, straight, one step at a time, without rushing. Imagine you're on a narrow path beside a precipice.

Once he's got the idea, you can vary the practice by getting him to back up between poles, round corners, or over a pole - he'll start to think about where he's placing his feet.

Getting him to back up is also excellent training if he tries to crowd you, shove you or barge at you at feeding time - your personal space is not to be violated, remember? Experienced horse-men will tell you that if you control his feet, you will control the rest of him. Now *that's* progress...

MOVING OVER

A horse which will move over to right or left on command is a pleasure to ride and handle.

- it makes him easy to manouevre next to that high log for getting on;

- gates become easier to open and shut;

- you can get past other track users without difficulty;

- you can keep his hindquarters from swinging out when passing other horses or when riding on the road;

- you can stop him crowding you when being led;

- on a young or untrained horse, you can use these cues to teach him to move straight, increasing his athleticism and reducing the risk of fatigue or injury.

An untrained horse moves rather like a tram: when you move his head to the left while walking, he will swing his hindquarters to the right. A bit unnerving when you're riding along a narrow path, with a sheer drop beside you! On a trained horse, you can move his quarters or shoulders over independently or together, which gives you superb control when picking your way through difficult ground or avoiding obstacles.

As usual, we start on the ground, before moving on to ridden cues:

Start this in the stable with the horse standing square. With a hand on his headcollar, apply pressure on his side near where the rider's heel goes with your other hand and use the verbal command "over". Horses often lean into the pressure to start with, but if you use a sharper, more "prickly" pressure the horse should move away. His reward is release of the pressure and a scratch and lots of praise. Daily repetition of this will help the horse associate the word "over" with moving sideways. Naturally, you should practice this from both sides.

Always start with a light pressure: if he ignores it, you can then make it stronger by degrees. Your aim should be to get him to move over from the smallest signal possible - once he is established, this can be as subtle as a pointing finger. If you always start off with a thump in the ribs, then that is what you'll always need to do.

Once he understands the basic principle, you can refine it by getting him to move his quarters only (turn on the forehand) or only his shoulders (turn on the haunches) by where you signal him - about six inches (15cm) behind the girth to get him to move his hind end, or on his neck (where the rein lies) to move his shoulders over. These cues will translate to the use of your leg (further back than the normal riding position) or the feel of the rein on his neck when you come to teach it from the saddle.

These are superb gymnastic exercises for him, but don't ask for too much at any one time - they are hard work for a young or stiff horse. Initially, he may try to evade this gymnastic effort by stepping forwards or backwards (easier for him). Be quietly persistent (of course), and be satisfied with a few quality steps to begin with. You can use a fence or other barrier to stop him stepping forwards or backwards until he gets the hang of it.

TYING UP

There will be times that it may be necessary to tie up your horse on your trips: going to the loo, fighting with a surly gate, going into a shop, for tacking and untacking, or while you get his corral set up. You may need to tie him up while you go up a garden path to a house for directions. Although this may seem a simple task, the potential for things going wrong is quite high: at best, a loose horse and at worst, a horrible accident.

In the equipment list you will see we have included string, a rope and advised you to have a headcollar under your bridle. This is the equipment you need to tie up your horse.

The string needs to be the breakable kind *not* modern baler twine, which may not break in an emergency. Traditional baler twine was made of jute which broke under pressure but the modern, synthetic twine doesn't and has resulted in cases of serious injury, even death. It is vital that there is a breaking point under strain.

Rider's Tip

Experienced off-road riders often have a loop of string or breakable twine on the headcollar – instead of clipping the leadrope to the headcollar ring, they attach it to the loop. This means there is *always* a breaking point.

How to tie up your horse

Always attach the lead rope to the headcollar. Never be tempted to attach it to the bridle as this can cause horrible mouth damage if the horse pulls back.

Use a quick release knot at all times so that you can untie your horse speedily if needed. The quick release knot is shown in the diagram. Ensure there is only 1-2 feet of rope between the horse and the string. A common problem is that there is too much rope allowing the horse to graze and move around leading to the horse getting his foot caught up in the rope or the rope wrapped around some other object and creating havoc.

On the other hand, don't tie him up so short that he is forced to hold his head at an unnatural angle.

Where to tie up

Even with breakable string you need to be careful what you attach your horse to. Even the quietest of mounts can take fright, pull back and take the object he's tied to with it, causing a disaster. So experience leads to emphasising where **not** to tie your horse first!

Avoid tying your horse to:

• Barbed wire fences	• Fence posts	• Bridges
• Sliding doors	• Cattle feeders	• Picnic benches
• Gates	• Vehicles	• Farm machinery

Most of these are dangerous because they can be pulled and dragged by the horse as they are not substantial enough. Also avoid tying close to strange horses, to avoid bullying or arguments, or where livestock may come rushing over and spook your horse.

More suitable places include:

- Strainer posts
- Trees (watch out for low branches)
- Walls with tie ring
- Strong objects that CANNOT be moved – do NOT underestimate the strength of a panicking horse.

Rider's Tip – Tying Up

Difficulty tying up your horse? You are not alone! Young horses are sometimes never trained, older horses have been given a fright and some wise horses have learnt that they can pull back, break the string and go off to have a picnic! What can you do?

You need go back to basics. You need your regular head collar, a long rope and a piece of string tied to your tie ring. It's a good idea to do this in an enclosed space. Thread the rope through the string and instead of tying the rope in a quick release knot you simply hold the end of the rope in your spare hand (wear gloves).

Go about some duties like grooming the horse, showing him attention so that he wants to be there. Having a haynet to eat can help encourage the horse to stick around too. If and when the horse pulls back, let the rope move through the string initially so that the horse doesn't feel pressure straight away. Increase the pressure and say 'whoa' until the horse stops reversing.

When the horse has stopped take him back closer to the tie ring. As the horse grows in confidence or in the naughty horse's case realises he can't get away, increase the quickness of the pressure eventually leading to actually tying a knot.
With plenty of repetition this should provide you with a horse that is easier to tie up.

NB Never leave your horse unattended when tied up and don't be tempted to tie your horse up with a pressure and release head collar.

The Story so Far...

Once you have established the 'foundation blocks' of getting your horse to stand, lead, back up, pick up his feet, tie up and move over as outlined above, you are in a position to deal with most of the hazards which may come your way. These foundation blocks' may take weeks or months before they are solid.

Basically you are now in a position to manoeuvre your horse where you want him, and the training time you have spent means a bond of trust will now be building up between you, providing you have been consistent in your approach.

This means each training step should always be a logical progression from the last one – you want to avoid asking for things which are currently beyond his mental or physical capabilities. For example, you don't want to be leading or riding him on the road before you have *firmly* established his 'move over' cues. It also means you should allow plenty of time when approaching something new, so you don't have to abandon the task halfway through.

> **With the skills outlined in this chapter so far we can now look at some common off-road tasks.**

INTRODUCING ROPES

More than most horses, your horse needs to be relaxed about ropes. Once this is achieved, you can lead him off another horse, use him as a pack horse, tether or picket him. You may not intend to picket or tether your horse (or indeed use him for carrying packs).

However, he should still have some familiarity with ropes – you never know when he might need to be led off another horse. Getting him used to having something trailing behind him will also help if he gets tangled up unexpectedly with vines or wire on the trail and is an excellent confidence-building exercise.

If your horse is calm with being lunged or long reined (even when things go a bit wrong) you are halfway there. If he hasn't had this experience, here is how to go about conditioning him to ropes. We like to use thick 'yachting' type rope for this – about 10 or 12 feet long is ample. The yachting rope is ideal because it doesn't snag or get tangled up in itself, as a cotton lunge line is apt to do.

The problem:

The two main objections that an untrained horse will have to ropes are getting them tangled round his legs or round his rear end, or a rope fastened to him which is trailing on the ground – if he panics and runs, the rope appears to be chasing him, and a wreck is sure to follow.

87

Rider's Safety Points

When carrying out the following exercises, wear protective headgear, gloves and sturdy footwear and work in an enclosed area: his box, a strong pen or a fenced arena is fine.

When you first start to work with ropes, do not attach them to the horse. That way, if he starts to get spooked, you can quietly drop the rope in a corner until he settles down again.

Exercise 1 – Getting used to ropes

With the horse standing quietly with a headcollar or rope halter and normal leadrope on, approach him with the rope. Let him look at it and sniff it, if he wants. Let him see you 'playing' with it – uncoiling it at your feet, picking it up and coiling it up again. Take things slowly and watch his reactions carefully – he will tell you if things are uncomfortable for him.

Working calmly, drape one end of the rope over his neck. If he is relaxed about this (hopefully he will be, as it's so far not too different from his headcollar rope), you can start to work around his body with the rope, draping it over different parts of him. Take note of where he looks uncomfortable (if he does) – this is often round the legs, the belly, above the hocks and under the tail.

If he starts to get frightened, you are moving too quickly – go back to where he was comfortable, and use less rope. The object is to habituate him to the rope, NOT to frighten him. It may take several sessions for him to fully accept the rope touching him all over, or he may doze off immediately.

He must stand still while you are working with him. Don't tie him up though. If he moves away, stop the rope work and put him back where he was, reinforcing the command 'stand', before starting again – gently to begin with. He must do what you ask, remember? If he is absolutely refusing to stand still, you may be working too fast or too invasively, or he needs more work on standing generally.

Take note of where he looks uncomfortable

88

You may wish to have an assistant in the early stages but your aim should be to dispense with them as soon as you feel confident. You will not have someone at your horse's head out in the countryside – he must be focused on you. In addition, another person there distracts the horse's attention from what is happening – a useful strategy when he's getting an injection perhaps, but for this work he needs to be fully aware of what's going on.

Giving to pressure

Once he is standing obediently and unconcerned by ropes trailing around him (and not before) you can move onto the next stage – getting him to give to the pressure of the rope. The reason for teaching this is so that he will not panic and pull back if he feels a rope around his legs, which can happen when he's tethered, or you drop the leadrope when you're leading him off another horse.

Again, ask him to stand still and square (to make it easier for him to balance). Wrap the end of the rope loosely around his pastern, holding it so you can let go easily and it will fall to the ground (ie don't tie a knot in it!). Using whatever word you use for picking out his feet ('give' or 'up'), increase the pressure on the rope until he lifts his foot. As soon as he does, release the pressure and reward him.

He may pull back at first with the unfamiliar feeling – just start over again, patiently and persistently, until he gives to the pressure of the rope in all directions. Be content with small moves at first and don't ask him to move his leg to the point where he overbalances, or is beyond a natural movement for him (particularly out to the side.) You'll know he's really 'got it' when you can lead him around by a rope wrapped loosely round a foreleg.

Repeat the exercise with all four legs (but don't try leading him by a hindleg...)

An extra benefit is that many horses will translate what they learn here to, for example, wire – so should they get a foreleg caught in a fence they will not immediately pull back, injuring their leg or ripping a shoe off. We once went out to catch our horses after an overnight stop in a strange field on a ride. They were standing demurely by the fence – it was only when we got closer we realised that they were both trapped by a particularly low bottom fence wire which had worked in between the back of the shoe and the hoof. Standing patiently waiting to be rescued, we were able to free them from the wire without damage to the shoe or the hoof, and continue with our ride.

Exercise 2 Trailing ropes

Initially with him standing still, make sure he is comfortable with the rope lying on the ground beside him. (Some horses confuse ropes with boa constrictors.) If he is, you can try moving the rope about with your foot – just a little bit at first! Once he's stopped snorting in horror, try leading him on a few paces while you drag the rope with your other hand. After a few paces, stop and reward him, then repeat until he is no longer worried.

He will probably be quite curious to begin with. If he is horrified at the very idea, you can quietly drop the rope while he settles down. Be persistent though, and he will learn that this trailing object won't hurt him, at which point you can try some corners, when the rope will touch his legs and go underneath him.

The broader benefit of exercises like this is that you have encouraged him to overcome his 'natural instincts' (of flight) and instead to accept your leadership (in this case to stand and walk quietly with a potentially threatening object around him, instead of running away.) Think how helpful this will be out on the trail, knowing you have a horse who is confident that you as his leader will keep him safe, whatever strange objects he encounters.

SADDLEBAGS

The problem:
Some horses dislike the feeling of saddlebags (especially behind the saddle) and this may encourage them to buck. Some horses are also spooked initially by the noise of bags made from materials like ripstop nylon.

90

On your trip, you will want to carry some items with you. Backpacks are not really suitable – you will find they unbalance you, as well as making mounting more difficult, and bounce about uncomfortably once you start to trot and canter. It is a good idea to introduce your horse to saddlebags before you actually set off.

The solution is again one of habituation, just like dealing with the rope. Start with him standing still. Show him the saddlebags, then put them in place (don't fasten them to the saddle just yet – if he gets upset, you can just slide them off.) Move them around behind the saddle, bumping and swishing them about gently until he accepts this strange feeling and noise. When he's unconcerned, you can fasten them to the saddle and lead him about, then lunge him (if he's used to that), so he can feel them moving about a bit.

Once he's accepting that happily, add a little weight and noise: empty plastic detergent or milk cartons are great, with a few pebbles inside to make a nice rattle. We suggest you hack out a few times with this arrangement: he will get used to the noise both of something rattling in the bags themselves, and also the noise of whippy branches brushing against them.

Rider's Tip – Saddlebags

When you come to use the saddlebags for real, you want to have a saddle pad which is large enough so that the bags are not directly touching his skin to give him protection in the sensitive area behind the saddle. You will also want to pack them carefully, so that soft items, like a spare fleece, are at the bottom – not heavy items with sharp edges.

CROSSING WATER

In most parts of the UK, you don't have to go very far off-road before you encounter a water crossing - and a horse which is unwilling to get his feet wet is going to mean some very short rides! Once he's leading well, you can use these skills to teach him to cross water. Many riders like to carry out this early training unmounted.

You will need his ordinary headcollar and a *long* rope - a thickish one about 8 - 10 feet long is ideal. We use this in preference to an ordinary leadrope or a lunge line: an ordinary leadrope is too short to allow you go get out of the way should he decide to do a huge leap, and lunge lines are a bit too long and have a tendency to get tangled round you. If you have a friend with a horse which will calmly and reliably cross water, they can be a great help and encouragement. Don't get an unreliable horse along though - you don't need Trigger getting any ideas! It's a good idea to wear sturdy boots and gloves.

Set Up for Success

Any fool can teach a horse to be stroppy about crossing water - that's easy. Just chase him roughly into a fast flowing, muddy river with a bouldery or soft bottom, preferably with a steep or undercut bank to negotiate - and see how amenable he is next time. As an intelligent handler though, you will naturally want to do the following:

- Pick somewhere safe for his first attempts: shallow clear water with good footing and easy gentle access in and out. Your local cross–country course may be of help.
- Have a reason for him to cross – heading towards home, another horse, or a bucket with a few nuts in it on the opposite bank if he's the greedy sort.
- Allow plenty of time. You know the old saying, "if you act as though you've only got ten minutes, it will take all day – if you act as though you've got all day, it will only take ten minutes." You musn't hurry this training, and time spent now will stand you in good stead for ever.
- Lead him up to the river (or as close as he's prepared to go comfortably). Allow him to stand and look, and sniff the water if he wants. Many novice horses gain confidence from seeing another horse in the water (or failing that, you).
- Don't force him into the water straight away, but don't allow him to pull back or turn away, either. There's only one way to go – and that's forward.
- When you feel he's calm, ask him quietly to take a step into the water, using the command 'walk on' and gentle pressure on the rope. Don't haul on the rope – he's likely to just pull back, and keep the atmosphere calm and quiet. You may have to be persistent, positive, committed and determined.   Be prepared for him to suddenly leap in.
- He may bounce across and out the other side the first time. That's OK, and he should be made a fuss of and praised. Next time, see if he'll stop in the water for a few moments, and maybe wade around a little to get used to the sensation of the water around his legs. Properly prepared, most horses seem to positively enjoy water. Once he's feeling confident, try crossing mounted.

You're not the only teacher – here a young horse gains confidence crossing water from his more experienced companion

Assessment Two – Ground manners (yours!)

- **Do you treat your horse with respect?**

- **Do you give him fair warning of a request, and time to comply with it?**

- **Do you praise him for an honest try, even if he hasn't quite got it perfect yet?**

- **Are you consistent in your handling of him, so he knows what to expect?**

- **Do you set up training exercises to give him the best chance of succeeding?**

- **Can you control your temper, even when things are not going well?**

- **Are your requests appropriate for his physical condition and stage of training?**

- **Are you prepared to seek help from someone you trust if necessary?**

- **Do you try to see things from his point of view?**

These horsemanship skills are not confined to off-road riding of course. If you can honestly tick the statements above, you are well on the way to forging an excellent relationship with your horse, one that will please you both over the many miles which lie ahead. If you're not sure, read on...

RESPECT

If you don't respect your horse, he won't respect you. He *may* do as you say anyway (because he's frightened of the consequences), but that's a different matter. Respect is part of trust and partnership and affection: it certainly doesn't mean you let him make all the decisions.

Respect is a state of mind, but it shows in your behaviour. It covers many things: making sure he is comfortable and appropriately fed; that he is kept in a way which allows him time off to just be a horse; that your communication with him is fair and as clear as you can make it, and that if you have to discipline him, it is short and as sharp as necessary, and you can then move on without bearing a grudge. It also involves listening to what *he* has to 'say'.

Horses respond to respect

If you often find yourself saying (or thinking) 'he's such a brute' or 'he's always disobedient deliberately just to wind me up', you need to spend some time thinking about your relationship with him. He *may* be playing you up - undoubtedly some horses are quite expert at this - but equally, he may not be clear what you want, be physically unable to do it, or he has learned that there is no reward for him in doing as you ask. For example, a horse whose rider consistently thumps heavily in the saddle landing over a jump and gives him a jag in the mouth with the reins won't stay enthusiastic about jumping for long.

The following sections also contribute to the idea of respect:

FAIR WARNING

This is a bit like a traffic light system: when you want your horse to walk on from halt, (hopefully) you don't just thump him in the ribs and then smack him immediately with a whip if he doesn't respond. If you've both been chilling out looking at the view, you would probably take up rein contact, straighten up in the saddle, close your legs and perhaps give him a verbal cue as well, wouldn't you?

The same goes for everything you ask him to do - prepare him, cue him and then give him a reasonable time to respond. 'A reasonable time' depends on his stage of training: if he's young and still trying to work out what you're asking, you would allow a bit more time than an experienced horse, who you would expect to respond much more smartly.

One of the areas where this is often seen is in loading into a trailer: handlers are often very keen to 'harry' their inexperienced horse up the ramp as quickly as possible (preferably with someone pulling from the front end, someone else shoving at the back and several bystanders shouting instructions), thereby setting up a reluctance to load, not just on this occasion, but possibly for ever!

AN HONEST TRY

Horseman Pat Parelli has a saying ' Reward the try' and it's a good maxim to keep in mind when training a novice horse. A horse who isn't sure what you want may try several things: your job as a handler is to observe the smallest move in the direction you want and immediately reward it with your voice or by taking off the pressure.

For example, you want to teach your young horse to back up on command. He's never done it before, so, although your ultimate goal may be to get him to take six steps backwards, straight and at a controlled speed, you wouldn't start there. Your first stage is to get him to take one step backwards, or even to shift his weight so he's leaning back, away from the pressure. Then praise, and give him a moment to think about it, before asking again.

By breaking tasks down to the component parts, you keep the atmosphere calm (and therefore conducive to learning), and it becomes clear to him what you're asking.

You can apply this step by simple step approach to **any** task, whether it's crossing water or retraining an older horse to lower his head carriage - **pay attention**, and reward each little step in the right direction.

CONSISTENT HANDLING

Horses on the whole don't like surprises (unless it's something they can eat). Consistent handling means not only using the same cues for an action, but expecting the same result (or better, as his understanding or physical abilities increase).

For example, if you sometimes let him lumber along slowly with his head two inches off the ground, and then suddenly insist that he steps out briskly in self-carriage, don't be surprised if he is confused (not to mention resistant).

This means you need to be clear in your mind what is acceptable behaviour (and then stick with it): if *you're* not clear, how can he possibly be? Different people have different expectations: if you've ever watched the same horse being ridden by two riders of different ability (or perhaps watched your instructor ride your horse), you'll know what we mean - sometimes it's hard to believe it's the same animal!

The skill comes in knowing just how demanding you can be and there are lots of factors which influence this: how experienced your horse is; how skilled you are; his physical condition at that moment and what other distractions there are round about are just some which might affect how firm you are. On the whole though, as you are trying to improve your horse, you will always be looking for a fraction more. This doesn't mean bullying him: it may require you to be persistent, though.

The principal reason for being consistent is that it is a vital element in building your horse's trust in you: when you are out riding in a strange and dangerous wilderness where anything might happen (from your horse's perspective - you thought you were having a day ride round the local forest park) he needs to be able to trust you. If you have always tried to be fair and consistent with him, he is far more likely to have confidence in your leadership.

BEST CHANCE OF SUCCESS

Like any good teacher, you want your 'pupil' to succeed. If you think back to a teacher, boss or instructor who has inspired you to do your best, you will probably find that they have some characteristics in common:

An inspiring teacher:

* explains clearly what you are expected to do
* encourages you
* allows you to experiment and make mistakes without fear of punishment
* guides you
* praises you when you get it right
* allows you adequate rest stops and time to think things over
* doesn't ask you to do things which are way beyond your current level of ability

Hopefully they also made it fun! Like you, horses respond better to this kind of treatment, certainly better than endless drilling with no feedback on whether or not you were getting it right, or worse, only negative feedback when you got it wrong (and you didn't know why...)

Horses may not have a large vocabulary, but they *do* seem to understand 'Good boy' and a scratch; or (best of all) you getting off them after a particularly good effort.

Other factors which may affect setting your horse up for success include allowing plenty of time for resolving any problems, as it's more difficult to be patient when you know you have to be at work in twenty minutes; and knowing when to stop. You may not have fully achieved everything you set out to do in this training session, but providing you have made some progress and are able to finish on a positive note, it is often better to stop and pick it up again in the next session. Horses often appear to benefit from time to think it over - animal behaviourists call this 'latent learning'.

Controlling Your Temper

'Where knowledge ends, violence begins'. Horses can be *immensely* frustrating to work with sometimes, but if you find yourself losing your temper with your horse, it generally means that you are overloading the training process with something else.

Could it be there's another relationship or other worries which are what's really annoying you (but you're venting it on your horse)? Perhaps you feel he's making you look incompetent in front of other people; or you feel he should be trying harder because you've just had to fork out for another month's livery and a new winter rug (horses don't think that way). Perhaps you're trying to do something which is currently way beyond his skill level - or yours?

Whatever the reason, there really isn't a place for angry people around horses. Whatever his perceived shortcomings, you (the one with the big brain, remember) need to find a way through it. If you can't do it on your own, *get some help.*

Note that sometimes, it is perfectly appropriate to *act* angry (as we did with Bart – see panel, next page). Acting angry with a pushy horse who constantly is crowding you is justifiable, if more subtle methods haven't worked. If he acts in any way which threatens your safety, on the ground or under saddle, he needs to know without a shadow of a doubt that that behaviour won't be tolerated.

APPROPRIATE REQUESTS

This means asking for things which are reasonable, given his stage of training and his level of fitness. If you've only managed to ride him for an hour a week during the winter, it's not ok to suddenly take him out for a twenty-five mile ride (even at slow speeds). He needs conditioning first (just as you would)!

For every inconsiderate rider, there are probably a dozen who don't ask *enough* of their horses. Time is precious for most people, and riding time is usually juggled in with a hundred other life demands. Many horses will improve with more work. With a little thought and planning, though, you can make the most of what opportunities you do have, to do something different and interesting and to progress.

Bart - A Case Study

Bart's owner came to us for help. She'd bought him for long distance riding from a riding school. In many ways he was perfect for the job - spook-free, calm, tied up quietly, solid and dependable.

Only problem? She couldn't get him to even trot without kicking for ten minutes first. His conscientious owner had had him checked by the vet and a chiro, his teeth done, and a new saddle.

Like many school horses, Bart had simply learned to ignore the aids. On he would plod, hooves in his ears, enjoying the view.

Sorry Bart - that's not going to do! We taught Bart (and his owner) three levels of aid: a polite request (gentle squeeze); sterner command (one kick - and that's *one*, not ten); and then the moveyourassnowImeanit command, backed up by a serious smack.

The sequence *never* changed. Always we asked with the lightest of aids. To begin with, Bart never so much as flicked an ear - he may even have slowed down a little, if that were possible.

On to the kick - again to begin with, no response.

The 'moveyourassnow' command worked - because we *meant* it. Didn't matter if he shot off in a trot or a canter, in good form or not - this was only about *forward*. He was then rewarded for his compliance.

Note: it's important that Bart was *allowed* to go forward (whatever the speed): the rider's body was kept loose and free - and absolutely no pulling on the reins whatever. Keep it simple.

Quite quickly Bart learned that, guess what, it was easier and more pleasant to respond to that first request. His owner has continued to work with him, and he's now a much lighter, more responsive ride.

We include this case study because it demonstrates some good principles: Fair Warning, Consistent Handling, and He Must Do as You Ask (provided it's fair).

Bart was given a structured series of aids that he could understand. It was absolutely his choice to ignore them, if he wanted - but he learned that there were consequences for doing just that.

SEEKING HELP

You've probably noticed that the riders who proclaim they don't need lessons are the ones **you** think would benefit most from them! You would hope that seeking out a qualified instructor would solve all your problems, but sadly that is not *always* the case. Again, you'll have to use your (big) brain and your own judgment. Some things you might like to consider:

Considering an Instructor?

Do their methods 'chime' with yours? Do you feel comfortable with the way they treat your horse (and you?)

Do they explain 'why'? What is the purpose of the exercise; why you should be a bit tougher (or the opposite); what exactly you're trying to achieve?

Do you finish each lesson feeling you've progressed and learned something?

What is their reputation locally? Everyone is entitled to an opinion, but this can tell you a lot.

Due to where you live, or for financial reasons, regular lessons might not be feasible. OK, you'll just have to be more inventive. Watch as many horses and riders as you can, as critically as possible. Note: by 'critically' we don't mean 'criticising' ('what *does* she think she looks like in those tight jods?') We mean objectively, using your brain. What do you like about the rider, or the way their horse is going? What do you *not* like? Why do you think that's happening?

Attend horse shows and events if you can (the warm up ring, in particular, can be very instructive). If you're watching a show class, what order would you place the horses? Did the judge agree with you? Many riding schools and equestrian centres offer clinics (sometimes with very well-known trainers), where you can spectate for a small charge. If you have the internet, look at some of the videos posted on sites like YouTube, but be warned - some of these are great examples of how *not* to do it! What would you do differently, if you were riding that horse?

Read as many books as you can, even if they don't deal specifically with off-road riding. Good horsemanship is good horsemanship, whether it's dressage, jumping or Western reining. There's a list of some we've found to be consistently valuable, in Chapter 11. By watching many horses and riders, you will start to develop an eye for a horse which is going well. You will see what looks harmonious, and which horses look definitely unhappy. You will be able to identify riders who ride quietly, in good balance at all times. Even if you're not quite there yourself yet, you will have a good picture of what you're trying to achieve.

Most of all, you will learn a lot, and that *will* translate into how well your own horse goes. You will learn to recognise short cuts, over-fierce training methods and rough, ineffective or unbalanced riding, and be able to avoid those mistakes yourself. No-one is born knowing how to ride - for each and every one of us, it's an ongoing process of steps: some forward, some back, and occasionally, sometimes feeling like giving up altogether...

THINK LIKE A HORSE

Your training will progress more easily if you work *with* your horse's natural instincts. The more highly trained a horse is, the more he will overcome those instincts - think of police horses jumping through fire, or an event horse which will take off over a fence when he can't see the landing side. At a lower level of training, a horse will happily hack away from all the other horses in the yard on his own - a reasonable request for most riders. This is against his most basic 'herd instinct' (stay with your buddies where it's safe). It's something which many horses object to - sometimes quite violently. You can use it to your advantage, though, by breaking it down into steps which are not as threatening for him.

In an ideal world, every young horse learns that sometimes it's ok to be on his own. Sadly this is often not the case: he may have run with other youngsters in a small herd with minimal handling, or he may have only had one companion, both of whom set up such a fuss about being separated that they effectively 'trained' their owner that *that* wasn't an option. Likewise, the older horse who plays up leaving home, frightening their rider, 'trains' the rider into agreeing with him that going out on your own isn't safe.

The more time you spend learning about horses and how they think and react, the easier it becomes to think of ways to resolve problems. Imagine you have a horse which is reluctant to leave the yard on his own (perhaps you don't have to imagine too hard?)

Hacking out on his own can be a challenge for many horses. He may stop still and refuse to go forward, perhaps even threatening to rear or running backwards. Or he may go where he's asked, but be so hyper alert for every danger that it feels like sitting on an unexploded bomb. Often he will be quite at ease if accompanied by another horse, so what's going on?

In the wild, 'a lone horse is a dead horse' as the saying goes. Away from the safety of the herd, if danger threatens, you are 'it'. Horses which refuse to hack out alone are generally lacking in confidence, which explains why they may behave differently with a very strong, competent, determined, confident rider.

If you don't think you're that kind of rider, what can you do? Horses sometimes become reluctant to hack out on their own because they've been asked for too much too soon, or if they've been asked in the wrong way - for example, a rider having been over-fierce when they've simply been nervous. On the other hand, a rider who isn't persistent and committed will soon be exploited by an unwilling horse. The best trick is to get him to a place where he **wants** to oblige.

Using the ideas in the panel, how might you train your horse to happily hack out on his own?

Thinking Like a Horse

Horses generally prefer to be with their mates.

They 'live in the moment' and react to the current situation, but have excellent memories, for example if they have had a fright.

They are very aware of body language.

Often, being asked for little steps which are immediately rewarded makes more sense to a horse.

They respond well to habituation – 'three times and it's a habit' (for good or bad).

They like to feel safe and comfortable.

They tend to respond better to a kind and patient (but persistent) handler than a noisy, grumpy or nervy one.

They don't like to be harried or rushed.

They are often easier to work with after they've burned off some energy.

We offer possible solutions over the page (no cheating, now!) These aren't the only ways - perhaps you've come up with something better! The important thing is to try and think about problems from the horse's point of view. That will make your training much more effective, and give you both confidence.

Hacking out Alone

Horses are often easier to work with after they've burned off some energy.

If you have a horse who is difficult about hacking out, don't just mount him in the yard, ready for a fight! Spend some time in the school first, getting him listening and co-operative first (or getting the nonsense out of him on the lunge, if he's that sort). Sometimes people come for help with their hack-o-phobe horse, but we find that basic brakes, steering and going forward are not established even in an enclosed space. So start there.

They like to feel safe and comfortable.

Find the level at which your horse is currently comfortable. He may be happy to walk out with you leading him, or with you riding him but another person on foot. He may be fine with another horse with him. He may be ok as long as he's within sight or sound of 'home'. This is your starting point.

Break it down into easy steps.

Once you've got your 'starting point' where he's comfortable, consider how you might make it a teensy bit more challenging for him, e.g. get someone to accompany you up the drive, but let him come back on his own. Horses find coming home much easier than going away! Gradually build up the distance he has to come home on his own.

If he's comfortable within sight of home, ask him to merely go another twenty yards or so outside his zone. You may find planting a bucket with a few nuts in it along your route gets him thinking more positively about the outside world (not always in the same place). He gets a reward before he gets ultra-worked up or upset. Letting him graze in a juicy spot is also a good reward.

Consider your body language.

Traditional advice often suggests planting someone on the road with a lunge whip to drive him forward if he naps. This may work, but isn't really addressing the root of the problem – to get him to be more confident. In fact, you've just given him something else to worry about/rebel against. Likewise, we don't recommend long-reining unless you're both good at it – it's easy to get in a tangle if things go a bit wrong.

Riders who have had trouble in the past may be tense, anticipating trouble. If you're also nervous, your horse will sense this (and think he must be right to be nervous too). Keep your movements slow and calm, your breathing deep and slow, and your voice low. Be prepared to be quietly firm though, with lots of praise if he is trying.

The fourth dimension

Time and patience are essential – you absolutely need to be prepared for it to take some time (perhaps weeks or months). When you set up the little baby step exercises, do it when you're not in a rush yourself. You need to feel that you've got all the time you need. Build up slowly: taking him for pleasant walks leading him, hacking home down the drive on his own, hacking up the drive alone but meeting another horse at the top, hacking out with another horse but going round opposite sides of a field so they're apart but can still see one another at first are all good exercises to build his confidence, depending on your facilities.

The Training Starts Here

- A horse or pony with good manners is a pleasure to handle and be with, as well as being much safer

- Basic manners you should expect include standing still, leading easily, moving over and backing up on command and allowing you to pick his feet up without fuss

- *How* you train your horse is as important as *what* you teach him, in order to build a harmonious partnership with trust and respect on both sides

- He must do as you ask - so be careful what you ask! Take into account his current fitness, his level of training and what's happening around you

- Seek help when you need it - don't struggle on alone, possibly making things worse

- Think like a horse!

The Training Continues: In the Saddle

5

Y̶ou may be thinking that off-road riding is the perfect opportunity to get away from schooling or training. However, a mannerly, well-prepared horse or pony will enhance your enjoyment and safety no end, and this is what this chapter explores.

Some off-road riders proudly proclaim 'but I never school, how boring'. They are often the ones with horses pulling themselves along, head up in the air and a dropped back, trailing their hocks behind them and making themselves more prone to injury or back trouble. Those riders are also usually the ones who use **your** horse's backside as a stopping point when their brakes have failed!

You don't need a purpose-built arena (much of the training can be done while hacking or in the corner of a field). You absolutely don't need a competitive dressage horse (in fact, some of those we know would have hysterics at the thought of treading in anything remotely squelchy) - just a pleasant, obedient ride, on which you can confidently explore the countryside.

This chapter begins by taking a closer look at you, the rider. We examine your riding fitness and position in the saddle, with several simple self-tests you can try out at home.

Are you fit to ride?

Now that your horse's ground work is going well, let's turn to you, the rider, before tackling the horse's ridden training. Riding for long periods naturally involves hours in the saddle, which can lead to fatigue and deteriorating co-ordination. We **all** have bad habits, and this is when they will show up worst! We can easily hinder our horse and cause him greater fatigue.

The following assessment looks at four main areas of fitness: endurance, flexibility, balance and aerobic function.

Assessment Three – Rider Fitness

Try the tests below, then tally up your score to discover areas of fitness which might need some improvement.

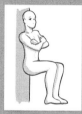

Sit with your back against a wall at 90°, legs shoulder width apart, feet flat on the floor and arms crossed. Feet should be in front of knees. Hold for as long as possible. (MUSCLE ENDURANCE)

>1 min – 10 points   45–60 secs – 8 points   30–45 secs – 6 points
15–30 secs – 4 points   0–15 secs – 2 points

Stand barefoot on a hard surface, feet hip width apart. Bend over at waist, knees locked and let your arms drop towards the ground. No bouncing! (FLEXIBILITY)

Palms touch floor – 10 points   Fingers touch foot – 8 points
Fingers touch ankles – 6 points Fingers reach shins 4 points
Fingers reach knees – 2 points

Wearing shoes, stand on hard surface. Stand on dominant leg, put other foot on its knee. Hands on hips. The test is over when hands come off hips, foot comes off knee, or when you move your weighted foot (or fall over...) Take the average of three attempts. Now try it standing on your non-dominant leg. (BALANCE)
Score yourself *twice*, once for each leg.

>40 secs – 10 points   30–40 secs – 8 points   20–30 secs – 6 points
10–20 secs – 4 points   0–10 secs – 2 points

 Walk briskly and continuously at a breathless pace over undulating terrain. (Use the same route for any retest.) How long can you maintain the pace?   (AEROBIC)

>60 mins – 10 points   45–60 mins – 8 points   30–45 mins – 6 points
15–30 mins – 4 points   0–15 mins – 2 points

NOW TOTAL YOUR SCORES...

<16   You may struggle over longer rides. The difficulty with being unfit is that after hours in the saddle you are likely to become sore, get fatigued and unbalanced, making things harder for your horse. You may also find your ability to make decisions becomes impaired as you get tired. A structured exercise programme, working on each area, will make your riding much more enjoyable.

16–24   An enjoyable regular exercise routine will help you to improve your general fitness. Set yourself achievable goals and stick with it.

24–40   Very good – you should cope comfortably with all but the most arduous rides. Did you find, as many people do, that one area was considerably weaker than another? For example, many people find they can balance on their dominant leg without difficulty, but really struggle on the other one, suggesting a body imbalance which will affect your riding. Identifying any weak spots will give you guidance on which areas to work on first.

40–50   Excellent – you should have little difficulty, providing you are also 'riding fit' – accustomed to using those muscles which develop from plenty of time in the saddle.

Whatever your age and current level of fitness, some work in this area will definitely help your riding and make your trips even more enjoyable. As well as hours in the saddle, you may be faced with lots of mounting and dismounting, walking for possibly long distances leading your horse, as well as having the stamina to see to his needs at the end of the day.
Even if you're not naturally athletic, you will feel much more positive and able to cope with the demands of longer rides if you're reasonably fit. Some suggestions for resources to help you are listed in Chapter 11.

Hmm – Could do better?

There are many forms of exercise that riders can do to improve their riding - basically you are looking to improve cardio-vascular fitness, posture, suppleness and core strength. In addition, an experienced, qualified instructor will help you work through issues on the horse's back.

Aerobic exercises such as brisk walking, cycling or swimming will improve cardio-vascular fitness - you will feel the improvement from even as little as three 20 minute sessions per week.

Remember that in long distance riding you will be in the saddle for a long time: you certainly don't need to be an Olympic hopeful, but the fitter you are the more pleasant it will be for you (and your horse), as well as reducing the risk of accidents or injury through fatigue.

Some of the best ways to improve posture and suppleness, release tension and improve general body awareness are pilates, martial arts such as T'ai Chi, or yoga. This type of exercise will also create **core muscle strength** - an essential ingredient of good riding.

Finally – we can mount!

How we sit on the horse (as well as his conformation and the type of saddle we ride in) affect our balance in many ways. Most riders are aware that what we *think* we are doing on a horse can vary wildly from what we actually *are* doing.

There are lots of reasons for this, but often they stem from a warped kinaesthetic (or body awareness) sense. By the time we're teenagers, most of us have adopted unconscious habits of sitting, standing and moving. We can twist, tilt, slump or have one side much more dominant than the other. Boy, do these ever show up when you sit on a horse, especially after five hours in the saddle...

To make things worse, horses will often mirror their riders, or adopt their own strategies for dealing with, for example, that seat bone which is digging into them.

Benefits of improved core muscle strength:

Stability If the horse stumbles badly or shies it is our core muscles which react to keep us in the saddle.

Independent seat Our legs need to be able to press, prod and kick and our arms need to be able to give and take on the reins without our seat becoming involved. Without strong core muscles everything gets in on the act.

Relief from back pain If you suffer from back pain when riding increased core muscle strength may help this as the stronger abdominal muscles take the strain.

Posture Balance, co-ordination and good breathing habits are associated with good posture – and good riding!

Remember, from your horse's point of view there is *no such thing as an inappropriate response*. So if he persists in running along with his head in the air and his back dropped, keeps drifting to the left when you're riding along the road, hates circling to the right or puts his ears flat back when you mount, he's telling you *something*. Your job is to find out what: it may be nothing to do with the way you ride him, but on the other hand...

Without a regular instructor, your best friend in assessing your own riding is a camera, or a video camera if you have one. Like true best friends, they may tell you something you didn't really want to know - but it's for your own good (honest!) You need pictures taken of you from the side, behind and in front, at halt and in motion.

 **When you have some pictures taken, compare them with those on Page 136. Can you identify your normal riding position in any of the photographs?**

So why is straightness and balance so important and why should we be well practised at it?

When spending a long time in the saddle we will undoubtedly be distracted by the beautiful scenery and the occasional bit of map reading, not to mention time spent day-dreaming.

Ideally, we should strive to be so well practiced in the art of straightness and balance so that it is almost second nature. If at all possible, help from an instructor on a regular basis will make what we *think* we're doing ever closer to what we actually *are* doing - brilliant!

On the next page is a self test you can use to think about your straightness and balance. It's worth learning this, so you can mentally scan your body every so often while you're riding – and see what you discover...

Self Test – How does it feel?

Starting from the head and working down the body:

- Is your head balanced on top of your shoulders? Many of us tilt our heads forward.
- Do your shoulder blades feel like they are sliding down your back? This helps keep your shoulders square.
- Is your diaphragm carried proudly up?
- Are your thumbs on top of the rein and the thumb nails pointing to the horse's mouth?
- Does your contact feel elastic? It shouldn't finish at the wrists but follow right through into the upper arm.
- Is your seat placed in the seat of the saddle and spread evenly across it?
- Does your seat invite the horse's back to come up to meet you, not squash it down?
- Do your legs softly hang from the hips and "hug" the horse? There should be very little inward pressure from the top part of the leg. Many of us grip with our knees and inner thighs but this perches us on top of the horse rather than allowing us to envelop the horse with our legs.
- Do the balls of your feet have an even contact with the stirrup? Many riders have too much weight on the big toe area creating a "knees in" position.
- Do your feet feel like they are resting lightly in the stirrups?
- Are your heels *slightly* lower than the toe? As your stirrups will be fairly long, this doesn't need to be exaggerated.

Sitting tall, square and relaxed isn't just for the competition arena (although sometimes that's the last thing you see riders doing there!) Work on your position over time will help you develop a secure independent seat, and allow you to ride for long periods without getting tired.

Assessment Four – Rider Ability

- **Can you walk, trot and canter in fields and tracks, i.e. open and confined spaces?**
- **Can you ride a figure of eight with your reins in one hand?**
- **Can you open and shut a gate on your horse?**
- **Can you rein back?**
- **Can you jump a small jump or ditch?**
- **Can you recognise good balance, speed and way of going in your horse?**
- **Are you confident riding in strange places?**

If you can do all of the above you're well on the way to a safe and successful day trip. If you have answered "no" to any of the questions there is a little more homework to be done.

Improving Riding Skills for Off-Road Riding

SPEED AND CONTROL

A great exercise to help with managing speed and control is to practice riding around fields doing lots (and lots) of transitions. Try and ride around 50 transitions in every ride. These transitions can be between paces or within the pace i.e. faster or slower in the trot or canter.

Fifty transitions may sound a lot, but it will have a hugely beneficial effect on all horses. The fast horse learns not to assume that he can just pull and go faster and heavier, while the lazy horse will be stimulated and motivated by the changes in pace. Transitions are an obvious way of communicating and are the key to maintaining a consistent pace in the future.

All these transitions have many other benefits. They will in time improve your horse's balance by helping to lighten his forehand and strengthen his back end. (In a transition the horse's lower back and hind quarters in particular are used, creating greater support for lifting the front end.)

They will also increase obedience - not just for speed but in general. Your horse will become accustomed to waiting and listening to you rather than being out there with his own agenda.

How to ride a good transition

You need to be consistent (of course) with your verbal and physical commands. Most horses seem to respond instinctively to the rider's tone of voice, so for a downwards transition use a slow, low, soothing tone and for an upwards transition use a higher, sharper tone.

Physically, no balance change should occur in either an upwards or a downwards transition, so no swinging around on the stirrups please!

In a downwards transition you want to give a series of half-halts on the rein (preparation) while becoming slightly static in the body to signal that the body does not want to go forward. Rigor mortis shouldn't set in - if you stiffen this has the opposite effect on some horses and sends them faster.

On the upwards transition use quick leg aids. The degree of strength will be dependent on his response - always start with the lightest possible. Remember to free your seat giving the signal that your body wants to go forward. Don't squeeze him to death - if you press for long periods of time your seat and legs press inward and downward against the horse and this will actually *reduce* the incentive to go forward. So keep it light and active.

If you do transitions frequently enough the horse will begin to "read" your body language and will respond more quickly. This will reduce the amount of physical pressure that you need to use with the legs and reins. Before you know it you will be able to maintain the speed with just body language!

So transitions, transitions, transitions…

STEERING AND ACCURACY

The use of poles in the arena help you become more accurate and help the horse understand the smallest of aids from you. The poles give you an aim and the horse a reason. The use of pole work is often forgotten but it has huge benefits not only for schooling but also to help the horse's surefootedness, as he becomes more aware of what his feet are doing. Don't worry if he knocks them or trips over them to begin with - he will learn.

For each session, lay the poles in different ways

These are just a few examples. Each pole should be approached at walk or trot at this stage, and they should be repeated over again striving for good rhythm. To start with you might find you rely on the rein predominantly. By using the same signals each time with reins and legs you will help him understand.

As you repeat the exercises, you will find a steady transfer of reliance from the rein to the leg. This could take anything from days to weeks to achieve and is an ongoing process. Once you feel confident and it's going well, try it with the reins in one hand. You will find an increased reliance on your weight and leg aids - and don't be *too* surprised if your horse starts going better than ever...

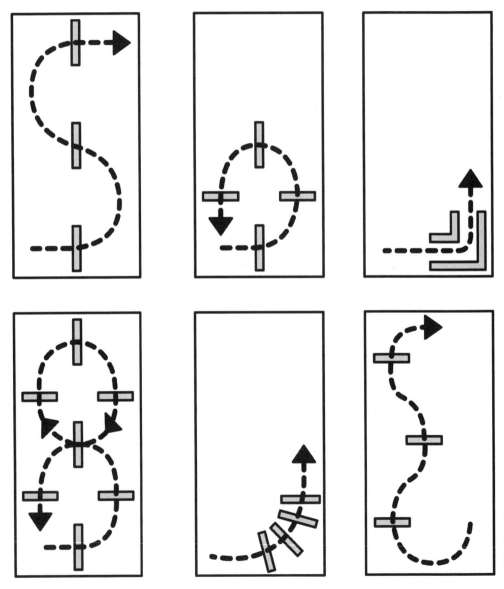

HOPPING OVER OBSTACLES

Poles are also the beginnings of jumping. Practice leading your horse over poles on a long (at least 10 feet) rope. Remember to stand well to the side of the horse with a good space in between you so that you don't get jumped on. Use barrels or blocks to support the poles so that you or the rope don't get tangled up in jump wings.

You will find it useful to differentiate between stepping over an obstacle and actually jumping it. Generally speaking, if the obstacle is less than knee high it's better to encourage him to step slowly over it (although some horses don't see it that way...) By stepping carefully, you avoid problems with bad landings, or upsetting the balance of packed loads.

There are lots of advantages in teaching your horse to step or hop over obstacles:

- You are going through the woods after a storm. There has been a lot of damage and trees have fallen in your way. There are a number of low branches making it impossible to ride over the trees safely, so the only way over is to lead the horse.

- In order to proceed along the track, you have to hop over a small but deep ditch but the ground on the landing side is very boggy. You don't want to burden the horse with your extra weight and lack of balance. The safest option would be to lead the horse over.

- It is also a great way of getting over an obstacle when you yourself just don't want to jump!

The magic carpet

This is a fun exercise to *seriously* improve your steering, even on a relatively green horse. Visualise the track you wish to follow unrolling in front of you, like a roll of carpet, or a thick black line - whatever works for you.

Using your focus only, stay on the track as it unrolls in front of you. To begin with, you will probably find it works best if you softly focus about ten feet in front of you: as you become more practised, you can unroll the 'carpet' further and further away.

Try some gentle turns, then a circle - following that carpet all the time. Can you maintain it at trot? Canter?

Many people find something almost miraculous happening: that where they focus, the horse will go.

Don't stare hard at the ground in front of you (that will cause you to stiffen and tip forward) - just softly keep the focus. You may also find you become much more aware of where your horse is falling in (or out) on turns and circles, or when he's travelling less than straight.

It's well worth practising this - as out on the trail, it's wonderful to know that you can steer your horse just with your focus and your intent.

MOVING AWAY FROM THE LEG

Once your horse understands moving over on the ground, you can then teach him to move over when mounted. A useful exercise is to teach him to turn on the forehand, where his front feet pivot on the spot, while his hindquarters move over, crossing his back legs through 180 degrees. This is a great help when manoeuvring through a gateway while mounted.

Classically this movement is taught from halt. At first, start with just a quarter turn and use the side of the arena or fence line as a barrier to help make it more obvious to the horse. Carry a long schooling whip and have someone assisting you from the ground in the beginning stages.

Start by riding the horse to the fence line and halting just before it. In this example we are going to move the horse's quarters to the right to end up on the left rein.

Moving away from the leg

At halt, have the whip is in your left hand and the assistant on the near side of the horse. Create a very small amount of left bend with the left rein. The right rein is used to half halt, to ensure the horse doesn't move forward. The left lower leg is going to move in a prickly, prodding way with the help of the assistant prodding with the fingers about two handspans behind the girth as well as the vocal "over" command.

When he moves his hindquarters over the pressure must be released as a reward. The right leg will lie passively behind the girth until you want to stop the movement.You can then apply pressure on the right side stopping the quarters from swinging any further.

Repeat this and eventually "wean" the assistant away. Practice in the same place until the horse seems to do it easily then move it to a more open space and finally doing a 180 degree turn. Do this training in both directions by reversing the leg and rein aids. It's fairly hard work for the horse – don't overdo it.

Rider's Tip – the Sluggish Horse

If the horse is sluggish to move away from the leg, use a sharper (not harder) leg movement. Carrying a schooling whip means that you can give the horse a light "flick" on the quarters to encourage movement.

To see how to use these techniques to open and shut a gate while mounted, see the photographs on page 137.

Leg yield

This will help you control the horse further with your legs. In time you will be able to alter the line that you are on with very little help from the reins. If you're sorting out your map and you need to avoid a bit of bad ground, pressing with your leg and positioning your seat is much easier than gathering up the reins!

You will also be able to prevent your horse from "crab walking" or 'lugging' into another horse with a press of your leg. Most importantly of all, it will give you greater control in traffic. There is often something at the side of the road for the horse to look or spook at causing him to shy over into the traffic. Being able to push the horse back into the side of the road with a press of the leg will prove to be a very useful tool for your safety, and stops him swinging his quarters out into the path of an oncoming car.

In leg yield we ask the horse to move forwards and sideways in a diagonal motion with his body remaining parallel to line of travel (i.e. his whole body reaches the line at the same time not shoulders first or quarters first!)

Initially it helps to have a reason to move over: for example moving from the ¾ line in the arena to the outside edge (where a horse will naturally 'drift' anyway), or from one side of the track to the other.

In this example the horse is leg yielding to the left:

The horse moves forwards and sideways with his body remaining parallel to his line of travel. The rider asks the horse to move away from her active right leg.

Her reins help to guide the horse, enabling him to understand what is required of him. The left rein (in this case) opens out to the left creating "space" for the horse to move into. It is also responsible for not allowing the horse to go any faster.

With her right rein, she asks for a very small amount of right bend. Her right leg asks the horse to move over with a prodding motion just behind the girth. As the horse moves over the pressure is released as a reward. The rider's left leg remains passively behind the girth. When she wants the horse to stop moving sideways and continue forward on a straight line she will increase the pressure of the left leg.

Note that, for training, she carries a long whip in her right hand. If the horse's quarters appear to be getting left behind in the movement she can give them a "flick". This exercise should be done in both directions with the aids reversed.

Rider's Tip – Leg Yield

Without moving your seat too much left or right, imagine the line that you want to get to then move your hips gently in that direction. Be very careful however of trying to push and "lift" the horse with your seat as this will cause crookedness in your position and tension in the horse's back.

REIN BACK

The need for rein back at this early stage is one of safety. If you step forward onto bad ground that you or the horse have not seen until that moment, you want to be sure that the horse can back up immediately. You may on occasion find you are unable to get the horse past certain obstacles or into water. In these situations a horse will often go past the obstacle backwards so you could well find it useful one day!

We started this training in the ground work section where we were using the word "back" or "back up" in different areas of the yard with the horse responding by going back. To develop this under saddle you will need an assistant on the ground for the first few times.

Choose a flat area where the ground is firm, giving the horse the best chance. It is difficult to rein back in deep going or uphill.

At halt and with your assistant at the horse's head:

Reining Back

Position yourself slightly onto the fork of your seat and move both legs back from the hips well behind the girth.

Open the reins to hip width and apply a *slightly* resistant pressure. Do *not* pull back on the reins! With your legs, encourage movement, while the assistant presses on the horse's chest and says "back".

As soon as the horse responds by taking a step back, the pressure is released. The rider resumes her normal position and walks forward as a reward. Repeat this several times with an assistant and eventually "wean" the assistant away with the rider taking on the vocal command as well as physical command.

The seat bones are lightened by moving onto the fork creating "space" for the horse to move back into and the reins create a resistance closing the "space" to the front. Be careful not to collapse your tummy in this movement.

Rider's Tip – Rein Back

Take care when doing rein back as confusion in the early stages can occasionally result in the horse rearing. Sometimes young horses can 'lock up'and seem unable to move. If he shows any signs of anxiety take the pressure off and walk forwards. Do more ground work and allow the assistant to do more until the horse has a clearer understanding.

THE HORSE'S BALANCE AND WAY OF GOING

We should endeavour to be aware of our horse's balance and "way of going" and try to improve this every time we are on his back. It improves strength and suppleness and helps him travel in a more economical way, reducing the wear and tear on his front legs and keeping his back from tiring and becoming weak.

The horse has four legs to stand on and at rest or in the field he will stand with 60% of his weight on the front legs or "on the forehand". This is fine as the horse is not being asked to do anything other than stand or graze. As soon as we start to ask him to do more than graze and meander around the field we add extra strain on the front legs, more than they are designed to endure over a long period of time. Circles, jumping, carrying a rider and trotting for lengthy stretches are not things you would see a feral horse doing.

This means that we need to encourage the horse to weight bear more on the hind legs to transfer some of the weight load from the front legs. This is often discussed as 'engagement of the hind quarters' and 'improved balance' i.e. not on the forehand. A horse that is in good balance is not only saving wear and tear on its front legs but is also a much more comfortable horse to ride.

120

Improving the horse's balance

This will come through systematic, patient and correct training - but don't expect it to happen overnight. The exercises descibed so far, in particular the work on transitions, will help to improve the horse's balance. Pole work also helps to encourage the horse to lift the forehand. (This can be developed to raised poles.)

Leg-yield also lifts the horse's forehand as it strengthens the hind quarters as well as the shoulder lifting muscles in the forehand. Plenty of hill work is a very effective way of building up strength in the hind quarters and helps the horse move "through" his back.

Hill work

Hill work should be done on gentle slopes to start with, working up to steeper, longer slopes.

The horse should not be allowed to rush up the hill and should be encouraged to work with his neck down, creating maximum work through the lower back and hind quarters. It will also increase the horse's heart rate and respiratory rate so it is a useful cardio-vascular exercise improving overall fitness.

Walking downhill has as good an effect on the horse's balance as going uphill. It encourages the horse to hold and prop his front end whilst sinking and holding his hind quarters.

Again, it's important he doesn't rush: inexperienced horses can easily lose their balance if their head comes up and their quarters get left behind.

The horse often finds himself going faster than he (or you) expected. If you lean back (as is often advised) that will exacerbate the problem. Instead, try and sit perpendicular to the ground (the way a tree grows), keep your seatbones light in the saddle and hug the horse gently with your legs, allowing him to make his way down slowly. It's usually better to go straight down, unless the slope is very steep, in which case don't be frightened of hopping off

Teaching your horse to negotiate hills safely is a vital part of his training

and leading him. Don't trot or canter a young horse downhill (whatever you may have seen in the Westerns): he doesn't yet have the balance or muscular strength to cope with a rider's weight. Even event riders or experienced endurance riders limit the amount of fast downhill work they do as it's hard on the horse.

On an unknown hill where the way isn't marked or there isn't an obvious track, it's generally worth following sheep/cattle paths as they usually choose the easiest way down.

"WAY OF GOING"

This is best described as the horse's posture in motion. Some horses naturally carry themselves in good posture whereas others will revert to negative posture, given half a chance. Some of this is due to conformation, physical issues or previous poor riding.

What is 'good' posture?

The horse moves forward from the hind legs, carries his back up, uses his stomach muscles and carries his neck in a soft curve in front of us.

The picture (right) shows a horse who has been encouraged and trained to carry himself - *not by the use of gadgets pulling him into a false frame - beware!*

This horse carries himself in balance, pushing himself forward from his powerful hindquarters.

The horse on the next page, in contrast, carries his head high with his back dropped. His stomach muscles are unsupporting. Conformation plays a part in this, but it also often indicates a horse which has been ridden with too much hand and not enough leg. This horse will pull himself forward from his front end, causing back ache and increased strain on the forelimbs.

This horse and rider demonstrate good posture: note the engaged hindquarters, the softly arched neck (with the poll the highest point), and the sense of the horse carrying himself. The rider is helping by sitting tall, square and relaxed, and looking ahead.

122

We are certainly not expecting the rider to have the horse
going "on the bit" for the journey. In fact most of it should be
enjoyed on a loose rein. You can work
on the horse's posture at home. Study
the pictures and decide if you are
going to have to influence your
horse into staying in good posture
throughout to avoid back ache.
Let's face it, most of us need to remind
ourselves to use our tummy muscles to avoid
lower back ache!

The more often your horse goes in good posture
at home in training, the more likely he is to
maintain it when out and about. Seek the advice
of an experienced instructor or physiotherapist if
you are in any doubt.

*A less harmonious picture altogether –
this horse's back legs are trailing behind
him, his neck is straight and stiff, and his
back is dropped beneath the rider, who is
tipping forward out of balance.*

RIDING OUT – PREPARATION

By working on the exercises so far, you are well on the way to having a horse who is obedient,
safe and comfortable to ride. He will continue to learn 'out there'. There are many new sights
and obstacles which are impossible to reproduce in the home environment anyway - not least
because he may be a little more excited or nervous than he is at home, at least to begin with.

However, you now have an impressive 'toolbox': you can stop him and make him wait; you
can steer him (and not just with the reins, either); you can manoeuvre him sideways to open
gates or avoid obstacles; you can hop over a log or ditch blocking your path, and you can back
him up on command. You've also accustomed him to ropes and saddlebags, so you're well
prepared.

He's working well at home, in the arena and out on hacks. You may be a little concerned
about how he'll react in a totally strange place - so we offer a couple of extra tools you will
find useful if you have a young or novice horse, or an older one who's a bit of an 'arena babe'
- lots of experience in the school or competition arena, but not too much mileage on the trail.

Until you actually try it out, you don't know how he'll react. However, the following scenario
is quite common on an early ride with an inexperienced horse:

> You unload your horse at a strange farmyard. Your horse, normally quite laid back, seems to have had a personality change in the trailer. He gazes round at everything, boggle eyed, with his head held high. He keeps snorting and whinnying, and you have to be quite firm with making him stand still while you tack up.
>
> Once mounted, he still feels tense. His head is still up in the air like a giraffe, he's still gazing round at everything in wonder, and when you move off, he jogs, snorts and shies at everything.
>
> You're starting to wonder if this was such a good idea...

Luckily, not all novice horses react like this - but some do! Is is any help if we tell you that a) he's just being a horse; and b) after a few outings, he'll soon learn to relax and conserve his energy? Hmm, thought not...

When confronted with something strange and possibly dangerous, horses will use their excellent eyesight and sense of smell to get a better handle on the threat. Remember when that tractor and boom sprayer suddenly appeared in the field next door? All the horses in your field cantered off, heads held high, with lots of snorting, before stopping at the other side of the field, where they continued to watch the tractor, still with their ears pricked, heads up and their nostrils wide. Having their heads up improves their field of vision, and the dilated nostrils helps them to smell better. The direction of their ears, of course, tells you where their focus of attention is.

In the farmyard, your horse is reacting in the same way - using his senses to get as much information about this strange place as possible. In this situation, as the responsible leader, your job is to make sure his attention is focused on **you**. With any luck, you'll also have your friend with their experienced horse with you for the first few times, and hopefully their calm presence will help your horse to settle.

Easy does it...

Generally, unless Bomber is being a complete idiot, it's better to get moving along the track, and not keep him standing around for too long, possibly getting more worked up. Start at a steady walk. The movement will help him settle down, and give him something else to think about. He will soon pick up on it if you are feeling tense or anxious, so keep your own breathing slow, deep and rhythmical, and your body relaxed and loose. You don't want to confirm his fears by gripping on like Robocop.

Ideally, you want to ask him to step out on a long (not a loose) rein. Make sure you're not gripping with your legs, but be ready to nudge him to keep him forward or straight. Use your voice to soothe and encourage him. Some horses will settle better after some *steady* trotting, if the track is suitable.

It's generally better to avoid getting into a major confrontation with him and escalating the situation (although you may need to be quite firm if he's being a bit silly). The majority of horses soon learn to settle down when they realise there's a lot of work ahead.

Riding Past Dragons

One of the best thing about going out in the countryside is seeing new things - unfortunately our horses don't always agree! Sooner or later, you will come across something at the side of the track which your horse is convinced will eat him. Sometimes, reassuring him and letting him look at the object for a minute or two is enough for him to decide it's not as dangerous as all that and he will move on up the track. If that doesn't work and he's still planted:

- **Keep him facing in the direction of travel – don't let him turn round;**
- **Let a more experienced horse or someone on foot take the lead (if you have one);**
- **With your legs and voice, encourage him forwards. Don't keep a tight grip on the reins – he may rear or start going backwards. He needs to feel you are *allowing* him forward;**
- **You may find it helpful to open your hands wider, channelling him onwards;**
- **Don't stare at the object yourself – keep focusing forward and up the track;**
- **When he takes even one step forward, praise him;**
- **Be prepared for him to pass the object in a rush.**
- **If he's still worried, you can get off and lead him past, keeping yourself between him and 'it'. This is when you will be glad you brought a halter and a long rope.**

You want to be very careful not to let his hindquarters swing out, into wire, a ditch or into the path of a vehicle if you are on the road. He will be focused on the 'spook' and oblivious to anything else. If a car is coming, stop and wait until it has passed before continuing.

If the obstacle is on your left:

Turn his head slightly to the right. This takes his focus away from the spooky object, and also helps him to see any dangers which may be on the other side of him.

Keep your right leg firmly on him just behind the girth, to stop his quarters swinging out.

With your left leg, encourage him briskly forwards. Again, make sure you're not

overtightening the reins and be ready if he speeds up past the 'spook.'

The Training Continues

- Improving your own fitness will help your riding, enhance your enjoyment, and make it easier for you both on longer rides

- Working on your straightness and balance in the saddle will make you more secure up there, as well as helping your horse

- Skills such as transitions, steering, hopping over obstacles, moving away from the leg and reining back will all help to make your horse a more manoeuvrable and responsive ride

- Paying attention to your horse's way of going will make your horse more athletic and less prone to fatigue and/or injury

- Be prepared for your horse to get a little excited on early rides if he is a novice. Working through the exercises in this chapter will help give you the skills and confidence to manage his behaviour.

These three horses are very different types, but all show desirable conformation for the off-road horse.

Each has strong hindquarters, a well-muscled back and a neck which arcs upwards and forwards from the shoulder – qualities which point to a comfortable ride and the potential to keep going for many hours over varying terrain without difficulty.

Physical attributes are only part of the whole, but a horse without serious conformational flaws is more likely to stand up to the work ahead, particularly for longer or more demanding trips.

THE TALC TEST
(See page 30)

Riding in a saddle having first dusted your horse's back with talc can tell you a great deal about saddle fit. Here, the saddle on the left shows full even coverage over the whole panels, indicating a good fit.

The saddle on the right has three bare patches where the saddle has not been in contact with the horse's back ('bridging'). This uneven contact means that the rider's weight is concentrated on a much smaller area of the horse's back, which is likely to lead to discomfort or even bruising. Note that the areas of talc are assymmetrical: this may be due to rider imbalance, the horse being more muscled on one side than the other, or a combination of these factors.

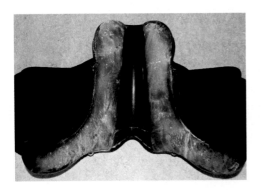
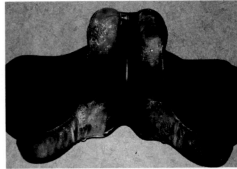

FENDERS AND CAGED STIRRUPS
(See page 31)

Articles of equipment worth considering investing in for off-road riding include fenders and caged stirrups (RIGHT).

Fenders are more comfortable against the inner leg for long periods than standard stirrup leathers, although they are slightly trickier to adjust for length while mounted.

The caged stirrups are an important safety feature, especially if you choose to ride in walking boots. There is no danger of your foot getting trapped, and the wider tread means you can adjust your foot position to ease tired ankles.

Note also the seat saver – a piece of equipment blessed by many an off-road rider!

BREASTPLATES
(See page 27)

TOP: A well–fitted breastplate is worth considering on your rides: it helps with saddle security (and sometimes rider security too, should you feel the sudden need to grab on to something!) The breastplate should follow the line of the shoulder and go neatly between the front legs to attach to the girth. It must not interfere with the windpipe.

In this close up, note that the breastplate is attached to the 'D' ring underneath the skirt of the saddle. This 'D' is attached to the tree of the saddle and offers a much firmer hold than the 'D' at the front of the saddle. This picture also shows a handy rein holder made of nylon webbing and velcro attached to a clip – useful for holding the reins out of harm's way at gateways or if you dismount for a moment.

This pony demonstrates a well–fitted neoprene breastplate which can help reduce rubbing because of the larger surface area.

SADDLE FIT
(See page 27)

TOP:

A well–fitting saddle sitting in good balance. The seat is level, which will allow the rider to sit softly upright, without being tipped forward or back. The panels demonstrate good even coverage.

CENTRE:

This shows a saddle which is too wide in the tree for this horse. The seat slopes downwards to the front, which will cause the rider to tip forward, causing unbalanced discomfort for both her and the horse. The panels are not in good contact at the back.

BOTTOM:

This saddle is too narrow in the tree, causing the seat to tip back. This will put the rider into a chair seat and will cause discomfort or pain for the horse at the withers.

PANNIERS

(See page 169)

TOP: A Shetland pony demonstrates that size is immaterial in a good pack animal.

She has a breeching strap as well as a crupper – a sensible precaution on smaller, rounder ponies, where the saddle may tend to slip forward going downhill.

CENTRE:
A home made traditional pack tree (Decker type).

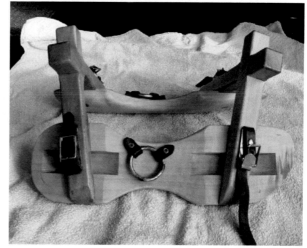

BOTTOM:

This bigger, broader pony carries soft panniers on a treeless saddle: a combination which works well for this particular animal.

Route finding with a map
(see pages 171-179)

You will see that the map on this page has been highlighted with the route in yellow - this is good practice and will make your route easier to find when you're on the back of a horse. Before setting off, take time to study the key or legend on your map, so you know what all the symbols mean.

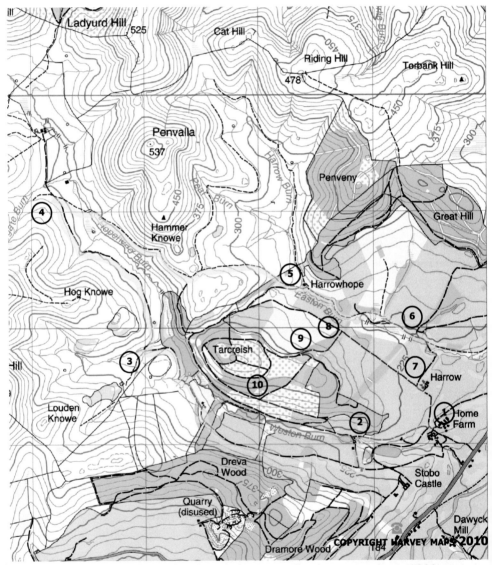

This map has a scale of 1: 40,000, so 25mm on the map represents 1000m on the ground. You are leaving from and returning to Home Farm (**Point 1** on the map).

Key to colours: orange is improved pasture, cream is rough pasture, dark green is dense plantation, pale green is woodland, and green dots are recently-planted tree plantation.

1.   Shortly after leaving Home Farm (**Point 1**), you come to a junction of tracks. This is the sort of place you can easily go wrong! Take the track to the left, and then the track immediately to your right. How do you know if you're right? You should be able to see improved pasture on your right (the orangey colour) and on your left, more improved pasture but with patches of open woodland (pale green). You should soon see a building on your left.

2.   As you approach **Point 2**, you will see dense woodland on your right, and then a cluster of buildings. Turn left here, crossing the Weston Burn. After approximately 400 metres (just less than 1 cm on the map) you come to a 'T' junction - turn right. This track (long dashed lines) is identified in the key as a 'track or forest road'. Follow the track for approximately 2 km through improved pasture, passing through a couple of small areas of forest. You may be able to see or hear the Weston Burn on your right.

3.   As you approach **Point 3** you will have open moorland on your left. The track turn sharply to the left and crosses a stream. You should be able to see a footpath (short dotted lines) heading off to your left at this point.

4.   Continue on your original track (which crosses open moorland) for approximately 1.5 km. As the track follows the contours of the ground, you can expect it to be fairly level. As you approach **Point 4**, you are looking for a point where a path directly crosses the track. Turn right here, onto a path. NB: If you find yourself crossing a stream (Margate Burn) you will realise that you have gone too far and missed your turning).

5.   Follow this path to Harrowhope (**Point 5**). You will cross a bridge over the Hopehead Burn. Note that there is no indication on the map that the bridge is suitable for horses - you may have to be prepared to ford the burn, if you haven't checked out the route with a land manager, access officer or similar beforehand. Again, you will be crossing open moorland. Note that the path splits just to the southwest of Hammer Knowe: take the right hand path here.

6.   From Harrowhope, continue following the path. You will have the Easton Burn on your right. After crossing a bridge, the track should become suitable for vehicles (long dashed line). At **Point 6** you will be able to see two bridges close together crossing the burn on your right, and on your left another track leading through an area of forest. When you get here, you will know that very shortly the track will be swinging right -handed, towards Harrow (**Point 7**).

7.   Point 7 is a potential *exit point* on your ride: if you or your horse are tired or sore, or the weather has turned bad, you have the option of a short cut back to Home Farm. When planning a route, it is a good idea to look for points like this, so you know what your options are.

8.   Your alternative is to ride another loop through **Points 8, 9 and 10,** before returning to Point 2 and back to Home Farm that way. Study the map and decide what you are likely to see on this section of the ride, and how you will know if you're on the right track. (Refer to the key below the map.)

The entire route (including the final loop) measures about 35 cm on the map: this translates into 14 km on the ground. Travelling at a gentle speed of 5 km per hour, you would expect this to take you in the region of 3 hours, not including any stops.

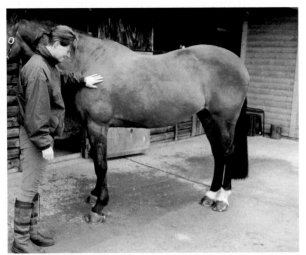

PICKING UP FEET SAFELY
(See page 80)

Having his feet attended to without fuss is a basic skill which your horse needs to master. It's surprising how many horses are difficult in this regard, either because they have never been taught, or because they've learned to get away with it.
Riders can help by:

giving the horse fair warning, not just snatching at the foot

standing in a safe place. It's safer to stand close to the horse, not at arm's length.

Picking up the front feet:

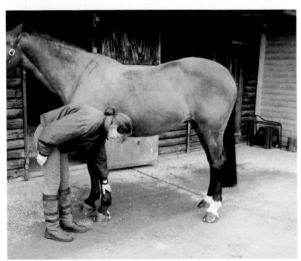

TOP: Start at the shoulder.

CENTRE: Run hand down to fetlock and tap it, giving a verbal cue like 'up'.

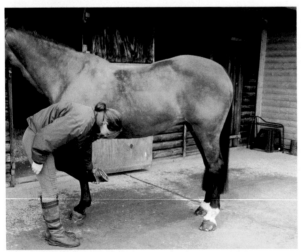

BOTTOM: Cup pastern with hand and lift.

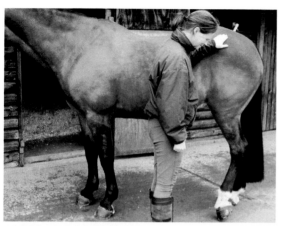

Picking up the hind feet:

Again, give the horse some warning, by patting him on the hindquarters.

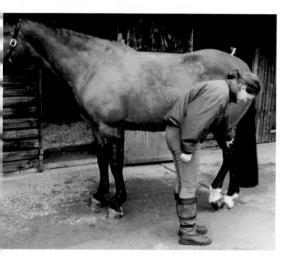

Slide hand down to the hock on the outside.

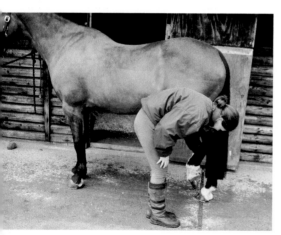

Tap the pastern and cup it to lift the foot, giving your verbal cue. Note the correct placing of your arm when holding a back leg.

Here the rider is tipping back –'the chair seat'. She is behind the horse's movement and he is hollowing his back, with his weight on the forehand.

In this picture the rider is tipped forward into the 'fork seat': a common fault which again is causing this sensitive horse to hollow and fall onto the forehand.

The rider is sitting in balance with shoulder, hip & heel in line. The horse looks much happier and is in good posture.

SITTING IN BALANCE
(See page 109)

It's very easy to find yourself getting out of balance with your horse, especially when you've been riding for some hours. Riding in a balanced position will make it much easier for your horse to carry you. Take a look at these photographs.

In the picture ABOVE, the rider is sitting off–balance, making it impossible for her horse to stand square as he compensates.

BELOW her shoulders are level, her head is balanced and her spine straight, making it much easier for her horse to mirror her good posture.

OPENING GATES WHILE MOUNTED
(See page 116)

Being able to open gates from the saddle is a desirable skill for the off-road rider. This sequence of photographs shows how moving away from the leg in the form of 'turn on the forehand' can help manouevre a horse through a gateway. The horse's front legs stay close to the gate while the hind legs move through nearly 360°.

You may find it easier to teach your horse what to do at gates from the ground initially: once he's got the idea, you can continue the training mounted. Make sure he understands the aids for rein back and turn on the forehand before you ask him to do it at a gate.

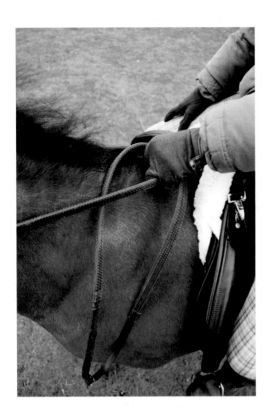

RIDING SINGLE-HANDED

(See page 172)

Being able to ride with your reins in one hand is a useful skill for the off-road rider: when looking at a map or taking photographs, or when leading a packhorse.

Both of these pictures show a rider holding the reins in one hand. Both are equally correct, but the top method allows a greater degree of movement and may therefore be preferable on a green horse which may need more correction from the rider.

When riding single-handed for extended periods, swop the rein-holding hand over periodically to discourage one-sidedness.

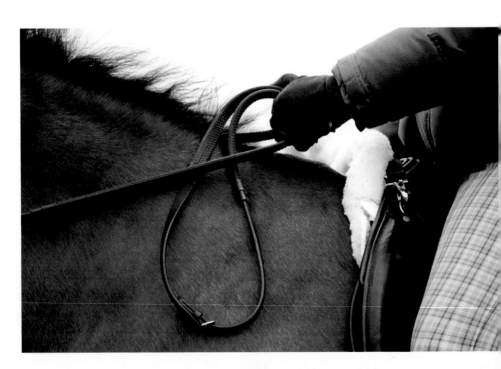

138

Assessing Condition

(See page 150)

Developing an eye for your horse's condition is an essential part of your management. These pictures show four animals at different levels of fitness. To a casual observer, the top two ponies and the bottom two horses may not look all that different, but a closer look demonstrates some key points:

TOP   This pony, a weight–carrying type, is fit to go. He has a strong hindquarters and back. His tummy slopes up and supports the back. The shoulders and neck are strong, appropriate to his natural build, but carrying little excess weight.

PICTURE 2 This pony is a similar type but is in unfit condition. Her hindquarters are sloping and weak, her tummy is unsupporting and she is carrying far too much weight on her shoulder and neck. She needs reduced feeding and increased exercise, slowly at first.

PICTURE 3 This thoroughbred mare is a completely different type to the pony above, but is in equally unfit condition. She has little muscle anywhere and is not carrying enough weight. She needs careful feeding to build her up and correct slow work to build up muscle.

BOTTOM This mare, another thoroughbred, has good muscle covering all over. Compare in particular the difference in the muscling over the back and hindquarters with the horse above. She is very close to a correct weight for her type.

PUTTING UP A CORRAL

(See page 207)

A lightweight electric corral will be an invaluable addition to your off-roading equipment, enabling you to safely pen your horse overnight.

TOP: The corral pack is neat and weighs in approximately 2.5 kg.

The contents of the pack include folding poles, tent pegs, 200m of tape and rubber bungees. There is also a lightweight fence energiser (not pictured) which runs off torch batteries but still carries a hefty 'sting'.

Whilst the corral can be freestanding, you can also use it in conjunction with an existing fence for a larger corral. Attach the tape to the bungee as shown.

Do NOT attach the electric tape to wire – this will conduct electricity through the wire fence and may also stop your corral working.

The corner of the corral, showing the electric power unit. Bungees fastened to tent pegs in the ground make a stable tripod, able to withstand quite high winds.

BELOW: the corral in use, with ponies safely grazing.

REMOVING A SHOE IN AN EMERGENCY

(SEE PAGE 226)

On a ride, you may find that you have to remove a shoe which has become twisted, sprung or very loose. The sequence of photographs show how to loosen the heels of the shoe after you have tapped up the clenches. Start at the back and lever under the heel, swapping sides each time.

If you can find a day when your farrier is not too busy (not always easy, we know!) it's well worth asking him or her to watch your technique, so that you can be confident you can cope in an emergency.

After releasing the shoe at the heels and working forward to the toe, the top two pictures show how to remove the nails from the heels and quarters of the shoe.

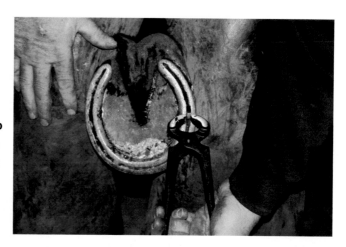

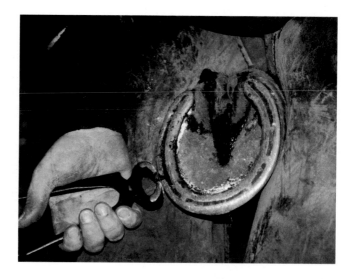

Finally, gently lever the shoe off, again starting at the heels and finally pulling the shoe off in line with the hoof walls, to avoid tearing the horn away at the toe.

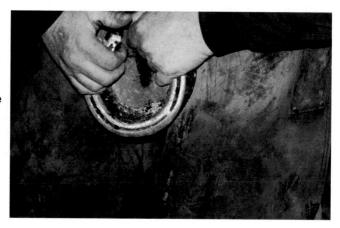

STRETCHES
(SEE PAGE 158)

Aprogramme of stretches will help keep your horse supple. Encourage your horse to co-operate using a treat. Don't attempt too much at first – regular stretching within his range of motion is far more beneficial than occasional attempts to push him through the pain barrier!

Neck stretches (LEFT) should be carried out on both sides.

Forelimb stretches (ABOVE) and hindlimb stretches (RIGHT) should be carried out on both sides. Note if your horse finds it easier to stretch on one side or the other.

TOP: Walking quietly past livestock ensures neither they, nor the farmer, get upset.

BOTTOM: Saddlebags loaded and ready to go.

"The breath of Heaven blows between the ears of a horse."

TRADITIONAL ARAB SAYING

Fitness and Care of the Off-Road Horse

6

Why get your horse fit?

The domestic horse does very little self-exercise even if he is turned out daily. All of his needs are generally within an acre or so - not very far! Additionally, his field is most unlikely to have all the types of terrain that you may come across: bog, mud, hard track, tarmac and steep hills. Even if you ride fairly regularly, one hour of carrying a rider and tack is very different to eight hours on varying ground.

The aim of conditioning your horse is to enable him to manage a long ride with minimum fatigue and risk of injury. The degree of fitness required depends on the length and severity of what you intend to do - but you will need to consider his fitness, even just for one day ride.

Being unprepared can lead to unnecessary injury to muscle, tendon and ligaments, not to mention the sores to the unprepared skin and the ache from the lactic acid that can go on for days! Apart from anything else, there is very little pleasure to be had from nursing a tired or sore horse home.

If we haven't convinced you, think about this:

We all know someone who has gone on a sponsored day walk unfit and unprepared. They have come home exhausted, blistered and achey for days afterwards. This is how your horse will feel only he DID NOT choose to do the exercise! We have a responsibility to be certain he's fit enough to return home in good shape.

Getting started

Your horse's 'service'

Feet

Teeth

Worming

Vaccinations

Physiotherapy

Condition score

Feeding

We like to start with the healthiest horse possible as this is essential to building fitness. Think of it rather like a car service. You wouldn't expect reliability without servicing the vehicle, would you?

FEET

These need to be trimmed and balanced and/or shod by a registered farrier. Normal practice is that shoes should be changed or re-fitted every 4-6 weeks whilst the horse is in work. However, every horse is different: shoeing too frequently may lead to the foot breaking up around the nail holes; not frequently enough and you risk your horse tripping or stumbling, as well as dealing with lost or loose shoes.

Help – my horse has poor quality horn!

There are several possible reasons for this - some genetic, and some relating to management.

The first thing to look at is his diet. Some horses benefit from being fed supplements that are designed to give the horse the necessary nutrients to grow good horn. Farriers Formula is one of many popular brands. We have routinely used biotin supplements for horses whose hooves need a bit of help, with good results.

Next, consider your management routine. If your horse is standing in wet bedding or a wet field it will affect the horn, as will long periods of hot, dry weather. Extreme changes in the weather going from very wet to very dry will cause the horn to expand and contract rapidly and this can cause cracks to appear. Allowing your horse to

To Shoe or Not?

Shoes protect the foot from the extra wear that riding will produce. If your horse can't grow horn at the same rate as it's being worn down then the sole of the foot comes in contact with the ground and the sensitive white line is exposed. If you have ever bitten or cut your nails down to the sensitive bit you'll know how this feels for the horse!

If the horn *can* grow at the same rate there's no reason why he can't go without shoes, as long as there are no signs of pain and you pay attention to getting off over very stony ground. You can always put on boots to protect the horse and take them off again on better ground.

Your horse will tell you if he is coping or not without shoes. If he's uncomfortable, you need to consider reducing your workload, changing the surface you are riding on or using boots. If you are thinking of going barefoot with your horse do this in "quiet time" as the horn will need time to adapt – this may take months.

spend time on dry ground if it's very wet or hosing his feet in dry weather will help. There are many hoof dressings on the market claiming to improve horn quality but used indiscriminately these can upset moisture balance of the hooves, causing more problems in the long run. Your farrier will advise you: ours recommend Cornucrescine for better, faster hoof growth applied around the coronet band, as well as in any cracks; and Kevin Bacon's Hoof Dressing for general hoof health. Your farrier will also be able to tell you if your horse has any bacterial infection which may be causing the horn to be brittle.

TEETH

Your horse's teeth need to be rasped every 9-12 months by a qualified horse dentist or vet. This will help the horse chew better, aiding his digestion. It also means he can move his lower jaw freely which makes life under saddle much more comfortable: he will be able to yield to the rein without catching himself on teeth hooks or abnormalities. Fussiness in his mouth when he's got a bit in or 'quidding' (when he drops uneated food out of his mouth) are both signs that he needs his teeth attended to.

WORMING

We recommend your horse is regularly wormed on a target worming programme. (Your vet or local equine supplier will advise if you're not sure.) Remember that he will be grazing on unknown ground on your rides, so it is worth doing even if your management at home is impeccable! Apart from anything else, you want to avoid bringing anything nasty (such as drug - resistant worms) home to share with your friends. It's good practice to shut him up in a box and worm him when you get home, too.

VACCINATIONS

Horses leaving home and mixing with other horses should be vaccinated against equine influenza annually (some places you stay may require evidence of this) and we highly recommend he's vaccinated with an anti-tetanus booster bi-annually.

PHYSIOTHERAPY

You may want to have your horse checked over by a physiotherapist or 'back man' before you embark on a fittening regime. This will ensure the horse has similar levels of muscle on both sides of his body and that he is moving in a level way. If there are any discrepancies they are better caught at this stage rather than months down the line when the strong muscles are fitter and the weak muscles are even more feeble.

CONDITION SCORING

This lets you know if your horse is underweight and undermuscled or overweight and overfed. Both of these will affect your training regime. There are two scales that are in use: 1-10, 1 being emaciated 10 being obese, 5 being ideal. The other score is 0-5, 0 being emaciated and 5 being obese, 3 being ideal. Make sure you know which you are scoring on!

Remember that a cob type will always look' fatter' and bigger than a thoroughbred or arab type but even the hairy guys do not need to be far away from the ideal score. There is plenty of information on condition scoring if you're not sure: the British Horse Society and World Horse Welfare both produce easy-to-follow guides. Remember you should be able to feel the horse's ribs quite easily but not actually see them. Weigh tapes can be useful and will help you identify weight gain or loss quickly.

The photographs on page 139 will give you a guide to what to look for when condition scoring your horse.

Feeding As we discussed earlier, the type of horse that you would choose to take on any long journey will need to be one that is able to survive on a mainly fibrous diet i.e. grass and sugar beet pulp. A horse that needs 16lbs of concentrate feed every day may require a packhorse all to himself! In this preparation stage your horse needs access to good quality grazing and a vitamin and mineral block. Sugar beet pulp is valuable as an excellent source of water and minerals as well as fibre. Prepared pulps such as Speedibeet or Readibeet are useful when travelling due to their short soaking time.

The Vet says...

"The natural diet of the horse is predominantly grass. He's designed to live on a fibrous diet. If you need only the cheapest and most convenient additional feed to provide energy and fibre, use sugar beet pulp.

Soaked pulp is also an excellent source of water and minerals. It's no coincidence that beet pulp is the only straight bucket feed to provide calcium and phosphorus in the same ratio as mature grass.

In this preparation stage your horse needs access to good quality grazing and should get a small amount of beet pulp if you're planning to use it on your rides."

THE EXERCISE PROGRAMME

With your service of the horse complete it's time to think of his exercise programme. We will assume your horse has had some time off or is currently in very light work. The aim is to put down good foundations for the future.

A good place to start is with a basic 6 week programme - the basic fittening for a healthy horse going on to do any type of activity. After 6 weeks the programme becomes more specific to riding off-road over long distances,

Exercise programme?!

carrying extra gear. Your horse doesn't need to be ultra-fit if all you're planning are some gentle rides - but it's unfair to make him sweat and puff if there are steep hills or a fast pace.

This is of course a guide: each horse is individual and should be treated so. Horses which have never been fit before will take longer to reach optimal fitness. Young horses' bodies are immature and will need more time to develop. The highly strung horse will be easier to get fit than the laid back, lazy one. If the horse has been off due to injury, more time should be taken at the walk stage.

Sample Fittening Programme

- ### SECTION 1 (WEEKS 1–4) PRELIMINARY

Week 1   Walking, start with 20 minutes on day 1 working to an hour on hard, level surfaces by the end of the week.

Week 2   Walking up to 1 ½ hours by the end of the week including some small inclines.

Week 3   Work should be at least 1 ½ hours and the horse should be working in good posture. Inclines should be used increasingly.

Week 4   A little trotting should be introduced on hard, level ground in 2–3 minute bursts. You should try to avoid doing this on the roads as this will be too concussive. Suppling work in the school can be added in for 20 mins before going out to exercise.

• SECTION 2 (WEEKS 5-6) DEVELOPMENT

Week 5   More trotting for a total of 20 minutes including inclines. Short
                canters on level, soft ground but avoiding deep ground. Increase
                schooling sessions to include walk, trot and a little canter.

Week 6   Trot needs to be increased to 25 minutes. Canter up inclines.
                Include some pole and grid work if you want to jump. Increase
                schooling sessions to improve suppleness.

• SECTION 3 (AFTER 6 WEEKS) SPECIFIC

Per week: 1-2 sessions schooling for an hour each

                2 long hacks which include varying terrain, carrying extra saddle

                bags and last up to three hours.

                1-2 shorter hacks that include steep hill work.

By now we are starting to concentrate on the specific requirements of riding off-
road. Your horse will be getting prepared to:

* Carry the rider for many hours
* Carry extra gear
* Carry saddle bags or packs
* Negotiate different types of terrain i.e. roads, soft ground, hills (up and
  down) and tracks.
* Drink and urinate throughout the day.

WHAT'S HAPPENING TO MY HORSE?

In Section 1:

The slight concussion of walking on the roads will cause his bones to strengthen and remodel.
Bone is a living structure which, when subjected to more stress, will become denser and
stronger.

153

The tendons and muscles pull and move the bones and they start to become toned in this period. Small amounts of stress on the tendons will cause the fibres to replenish themselves creating younger, stronger fibres which are more able to cope with stress and strain.

Trotting needs to be done on soft (not deep) ground: trotting on roads at this stage will jar joints and may cause damage. Your horse's heart rate will increase when he trots so the heart will start to become stronger and the lungs more efficient. This trot work will also stimulate unused capillaries back into use.

In Section 2:

Canter work will continue to develop his heart and lung fitness. It is also good for building up muscle. In canter the horse moves asymmetrically i.e. when he canters with right canter lead he uses different muscles than when he canters with left canter lead. You need to do equal amounts of both canter leads to help build up a level horse.

Schooling the horse means we can get on with the suppling and pole exercises that were discussed in the previous chapter.

In Section 3:

The long back muscle
(longissimus dorsi).

This will be subjected to long periods of time carrying your weight, plus the weight of the saddle and packs. It is also involved in propelling the horse forward as the power from the horses 'engine' in the hindquarters ripples forwards through the horse's back. (This is particularly noticeable when the horse is going uphill.)

In order for this to become stronger, your horse needs to work slowly for longer periods of time so that the muscle fibres undergo small amounts of stress encouraging them to replace fibres with younger, stronger ones.

It is endurance of muscle we need - which is why we can take it slowly. The horse should work in good posture to build up best and most appropriate muscle. Spending time carrying the extra saddle packs will expose his skin to some wear. The skin's response to this wear will be to thicken in that area. If this is done slowly and the packs are of good quality and fit well this should ensure the horse does not get sore.

Schooling sessions still need to be included as they will help keep the horse supple. When the horse becomes increasingly fit it is easy for his body to become stiff, as you will know if you have ever trained for long-distance walking or running. Keeping him as supple as possible will help minimise the risk of injury.

Riding for small amounts of time on different terrain helps the body make small changes to bone, ligament, tendon and muscle to become younger and stronger. None of this should be done at speed or in excess - you're not trying to cause strain-type injuries.

To encourage the inexperienced horse to drink and urinate during the day in strange places is easier said than done for some! It's useful to go out on some long hacks with a more experienced companion which is used to doing both. Horses are great copiers.

It's also helpful if you can recognise when he needs to 'go'. He may try to get off the hard track or road (horses don't like splashing their legs) or slowing up repeatedly or straddling. Some horses refuse to urinate with a rider on board, so be prepared to hop off if necessary.

CARE AND MANAGEMENT OF THE HORSE

There are specific things to look out for in preparation, during and after the trips. On the next page is a quick reminder of what to look for.

Taking his temperature

Use a veterinary thermometer. Shake it well before use (only necessary if it's a mercury one). Lightly grease the bulb end with Vaseline. Don't grease the end you hold, for obvious reasons!

Stand to the side of the horse's hind quarters and lift the tail. Insert the thermometer into the horse's rectum with a slight twisting action until it is fully in with only enough left for you to hold on to. Press it to the side so that it touches the wall of the rectum and hold for 1-2 minutes. Remember not to let go...

Finally remove with a slight twisting action and read. Digital thermometers are easier to read.

Signs of good health

- **Normal Greeting** A normal (for him) greeting will often tell you if your horse is feeling well or not.
- **Alert expression** Eyes and ears should follow movement in the field and yard. If he's uninterested in his surroundings he may be feeling under the weather.
- **Shiny, flat coat** If his coat looks dull and 'starey' then he's not in great health.
- **Skin loose and supple** This lets you know he's hydrated and eating and drinking correctly
- **No patchy sweat** Patchy sweat is an indicator of distress or discomfort.
- **Eyes, ears and nose** These should be clear of any discharge. The eyes should be open equally.
- **Eating and drinking** Going off his food or drink should alert you that there is something wrong that needs further observation and investigation.
- **Lumps and bumps** – Know your horse's body and legs and run your hands all over. Heat, lumps and bumps may indicate bruising, injury or allergy.
- **Stance** It is normal for the horse to rest a hind leg and occasionally change the resting leg. He shouldn't be resting a front leg or continually be shifting weight from one to the other. This indicates discomfort in the front leg or legs.
- **Urine** This should be clear or light yellow and passed several times a day. If it becomes dark and thick then this can be a sign of dehydration. If it becomes dark red or black looking your horse is need of veterinary attention promptly.
- **Droppings** These should form balls and break up on hitting the ground. The colour is dependent on what the horse is eating and they may be looser on rich grass, but they shouldn't look like cow pats!
- **Rolling** It is normal for a horse to have a roll or two but not normal to be continually getting up and down to roll repeatedly. This is one of the signs of colic and the horse needs veterinary attention urgently.
- **Mucous membranes** These are the gums, the inside of his nostrils and under the eye lids. They should be salmon pink in colour. Get to know your horse's.
- **Normal Temperature, Pulse and Respiration** It's good to know your horse's normal T P R. Increased pulse and respiration ar rest may indicate some form of distress or discomfort. Deviations in temperature indicate illness and the need for veterinary attention. Normal parameters are:

Temperature – 38 degrees C (100–101 degrees F)
Pulse – 36–42 beats per minute at rest
Respiration – 6 - 18 Inhalations per minute at rest

156

Taking his pulse

The easiest place to take the pulse is inside the left cheek bone:

If you move the skin around in this area you will come across something that feels like an earthworm under the skin. This is the facial artery.

With your first two fingers press this vessel against the cheek bone and try to feel a pulse - it will seem slow at rest.

Count the pulse for 15 seconds and multiply by 4 to calculate the beats per minute.

Respiration

Stand behind and to the side of the horse and watch the flanks rise and fall. A combination of in and out is counted as one. Count the inhalations for a minute.

Feeding

As discussed earlier, hopefully you have a horse that thrives well on little extra feeding. He should have access to a vitamin and mineral block and if you have not already started to feed sugar beet pulp then you can introduce this now.

In preparation for the trip it's helpful to feed sugar beet pulp in the form of one of the rapid-soaking varieties, such as Speedi Beet. On your trip, Speedi Beet can be transported dry and soaked at the end or the beginning of the day when you have access to water - it's ready in around 10 minutes unlike regular sugar beet pulp which must be soaked for at least twelve hours. Start feeding it *before* your trip - a horse's digestive system doesn't like sudden changes.

Start by feeding a small amount, gradually increasing to your required amount. This allows his system to adjust to the new food and build up enough bacteria to get the most from the food. The natural sugar content makes it tasty and because of this it can be an excellent way of getting much needed water into fussy drinkers.

Rider's Tip – Speedi Beet

Speedi Beet is a specially-prepared form of sugar beet pulp and should not be confused with the regular pulp that comes in the form of shreds or nuts. These need to be soaked for 12 hours (shreds) and 24 hours (nuts) : they are DANGEROUS if fed before these times.

Feet

It's most practical to have your horse shod a week before the trip. This allows the shoes to settle in and allow for any problems such as tight nails or nail bind to show up. At a week old the shoes will still have plenty if wear and grip and the feet will have been balanced and will still be balanced at this stage reducing any risk of injury. Practice using your hoof boots before you leave so that you are not fumbling around figuring out how to work them on the side of a hill. There are a number of different shoeing possibilities for long trips, such as road nails, borium tips etc. For a trip of two weeks or less, these are unlikely to be necessary.

Physiotherapy

In the run up to going away it's helpful to have a physiotherapist to look over your horse. They will be able to identify any weak or tight spots that have arisen during the fittening programme. A good physio will also be able to show you any specific stretches or massage techniques which are relevant to your particular horse. These might be for both pre- and post-exercise and will be of great benefit to your horse on any lengthy journey.

Sample 5 minute rub down

Before turning your horse out you can give him a rub and stretch to help any tired muscles.

Start with effleurage. This is when you rub the horse with the flat of your hand in long stroking motion which is over-lapping. The pressure is light to medium. Follow the contours of the horse over the neck, shoulders, back, hindquarters and hamstrings.

Then go on to kneading the main muscle areas i.e. the shoulders, gluteals and lumber muscles. This is done with your fingers closed and thumb sticking out. The knuckles are what make contact and this is done with more pressure than the effleurage.

You can if you wish rub arnica gel over the back and hamstrings. Arnica gel passes through the skin and helps ease bruising in tired muscles.

Stretches for the neck and back known as 'carrot stretches' will keep the horse supple. Do this with a little food to encourage the horse to turn his head towards his girth area aiming to get to the hip when the horse is super supple! Do this to both sides of the horse. You should also encourage him to drop his head to between his knees.

Lastly, some leg stretches:

Forelimb protraction: Lift the horse's front leg forwards with as straight a knee as possible.

Forelimb retraction: Lift the horses leg back with his knee at an angle of 90°.

Hindlimb protraction: Lift the hind leg pointing the toe towards the tendons of the front leg.

There are photographs demonstrating these stretches on page 144.

Flies and midges

Uncontrolled, these can create misery for you and your horse in the summer months. In general, they are less troublesome while you're actually moving, but can cause real distress when you stop.

In general, it's preferable to leave your horse's mane and tail as long as possible if you can - this is his natural defence. For sensitive horses, consider carrying a face and ear mask which you can pop on when you stop which will make him more comfortable - you can even ride with it on if the insects are really troublesome, but be aware his vision may be slightly impaired (so don't go jumping stone walls.)

Try different products before you leave to find out what works for you and your horse. There are many deterrents on the market, ranging from products containing DEET or pyrethrin/pymethrin to plant-based remedies - your choice is likely to be guided on how you feel about using synthetic chemicals on your horse.

Plant-based deterrents are likely to contain some of the following: eucalyptus, citronella, tea tree, lavender, lemon, clove bud, cedarwood, garlic, rosemary, peppermint, thyme, neem oil. Many riders believe feeding garlic supplements to their horses reduces fly problems.

There is currently no legal requirement – beyond the advertising laws that apply to everything sold in the UK – for manufacturers to prove the efficacy of active ingredients in equine insect repellents - so there is a degree of trial and error.

Where possible, arrange your rest stops en route on open ground, away from trees and standing water. Higher ground also is likely to offer more of a breeze (if not a positively brisk wind) which keeps insects away.

Ticks

These can be particularly troublesome in upland areas between April and October, although they rarely cause problems in horses other than mild irritation around the face and ears, and occasionally the lower limbs.

Ticks cannot hop or fly, but climb up grass or bracken and then latch on to limbs, lips, the muzzle or ears of passing animals. Adult ticks then spend several days feeding and their bodies become engorged with blood.

The majority of British horses appear to mount an effective immune response to infection and only a handful become sick. However, there is a small possibility of them contracting Lyme disease, which is associated with a variety of symptoms in horses, from mild depression and loss of interest in food, to weight loss, arthritis, inflammation of the eyes (uveitis), and neurological signs including behavioural changes and paralysis.

This range of clinical signs, which can also be caused by a number of other common equine conditions, does make it difficult to diagnosis Lyme disease (Borreliosis). Affected horses are often treated for the more common causes of weight loss, arthritis or uveitis, and it is only when treatment fails that the possibility of Lyme disease is considered. A definitive diagnosis relies upon detecting the presence of Borrelia burgdorferi bacteria in blood, urine or joint fluid using a sensitive DNA test.

There is no vaccine for Lyme disease, so frequent removal of ticks from horses is advisable. The most practical and effective method of tick removal is to use a special tick removing tool like the O'Tom Tick Twister and the Trix Tick Lasso. These are inexpensive and designed so that the tick is removed in its entirety, including mouth parts, and are available from vets, pet shops or at the tick prevention week website (see below). Simply pulling ticks off tends to leave the mouth parts behind, which can become infected.

In heavily tick-infested areas, we have resorted to rubbing oil or grease onto the lower limbs and muzzle. For more information about ticks, see the website **www.tickpreventionweek.org** run by the charity BADA-UK (Borreliosis and Associated Diseases Awareness-UK) which has lots of information about ticks, including how to deter and remove them .

Tack

Make sure that your bridle is fitting well and is well oiled as supple tack causes fewer rubs than hard un-oiled leather. Make sure that the saddle still fits, as your horse may have changed shape as he's got fitter. After riding each day check the sweat patches in the saddle area and see if they are similar on both sides. Uneven sweating can indicate uneven saddle pressure.

Rider's Tip – Hardening Skin

WARNING: TEST A SMALL AREA OF SKIN (WHICH IS NOT IN CONTACT WITH TACK OR SADDLEBAGS) AND WAIT A DAY OR TWO, IN CASE OF ALLERGY.

Hardening up certain areas of skin:
If your horse is prone to skin sores (often under the girth or behind the saddle), there are a couple of remedies you can try:

dissolve two teaspoons of salt in a pint of warm water and apply it
some riders prefer to use toilet soap, then surgical spirit, and finally sprinkle some talcum powder on areas which are prone to getting sore.

Many 'old timers' use human urine (yes, really). Urine contains urea and lots of other different metabolised chemicals, which will harden up the skin. Urine from a healthy person is sterile.

If your horse already has developed a skin sore:
Dab it with salty warm water, and keep it clean. Infected sores may require veterinary attention.

Fitness and Care of the Off-Road Horse

- Most horses and ponies will benefit from improved fitness, which will help them cope with being ridden for longer periods than usual

- Giving your horse a 'service' before you start any exercise programme will ensure you are starting from the best possible baseline

- A sample fittening programme is contained within this chapter. Make sure you start slowly, to allow your horse's body time to adjust

- Get to know what's normal for your horse - and be alert for any changes. Learn the signs of good health, and how to monitor your horse

- Plan how you are going to deal with insects and other irritants on your rides, to help keep your horse comfortable.

Using a Packhorse

7

Have you ever secretly dreamed of being a cowboy? To set off for the horizon with everything you need to be self-sufficient is many an off-road rider's dream. The flexibility to be able to set up camp anywhere is one of the joys of this kind of travel — (for some: others are rather keener on the hot bath and a nearby bar method!)

Increasingly popular in the UK is journeying on foot, using a packhorse to carry all the gear - a great job for an outgrown pony. Thoughtfully loaded, he can carry the necessary equipment for two or three people.

Using a packhorse means you can carry everything you need for you and your horses, and makes it practical to carry items such as an electric corral and extra feeding for your horses (and you!) However, adding a packhorse requires extra skills and vigilance on your part, as there is now twice as much to go wrong.

This chapter explains the merits (and otherwise) of using a packhorse and what sort of animal is suitable for this job. It also explains what additional equipment you will need, and how to set about training, loading, and manoeuvring your additional companion.

The Pros and Cons of Using a Packhorse

There are many advantages to having a packhorse with you, particularly if you are travelling through remote areas and intend to be as self-sufficient as possible. If you're intending to camp, a packhorse is pretty well essential to carry all the additional gear, unless you're a hardy type who will willingly nestle down in a bivvy bag in the open air. However, taking a packhorse with you is not without its own considerations.

Advantages:

- You can carry considerably more weight, and thus be much more self-sufficient
- If you're riding alone, horses are generally more confident on the trail and more settled at night and during rest stops if they have a companion, and less likely to wander
- If you're riding with others, two or perhaps three of you can share the same packhorse – you don't need one each

Disadvantages

- You will definitely be slower. It's unfair to ask a packhorse to go faster than a gentle trot. In addition, you will lose a lot of time manoeuvring through gates and round other obstacles
- It's twice the work at the beginning and end of the day (when you may be very tired): grooming, saddling, feeding etc.
- You need much more room. A pedestrian-type gate or narrow bridge which would present no problem to your ridden horse may mean you have to unload your packhorse
- You need excellent control when riding on the road (see below)
- Kitting out your packhorse will probably involve you in added expense

A suitable candidate

An unsuitable packhorse will make your off-road excursions uncomfortable at best and a nightmare at worst, so what do you need to look for?

Broadly speaking, you are looking for the same sort of characteristics as you would in a ridden horse: excellent feet, reasonable conformation and good manners. From experience, the calmer and more phlegmatic individuals often make good pack animals – the sort who won't panic or bolt when you drop the lead rope (as you will) or if the load begins to slip.

It can be an excellent job for a horse or pony who for whatever reason is not a great riding prospect: outgrown children's ponies you can't bear to part with; an older horse who might find carrying an adult rider all day too much, but can carry a lighter, thoughtfully-packed load without difficulty; or an animal who is just not comfortable to ride for hours, due perhaps to being very wide or having a choppy stride.

It's also a great job for younger animals (not less than four though) who are a 'work in progress' as far as their ridden training is going. Getting out and about in the countryside with a more experienced companion will benefit them in many ways, provided that the training detailed below is well established.

The ideal packhorse:

* has similar paces to your ridden horse (gorilla arms from tugging at him all day to keep up is never a good look)

* likewise, gets on reasonably well with your ridden horse. The animals often need to be physically close to one another – tricky when one of them is frightened of being kicked or bitten. Having said that, horses which are not particularly friendly in the field are quite likely to get on better away from home, especially if it's just the two of them.

* is fairly obedient by nature, as you will have to control him from a distance. In particular, he needs to be very responsive to leading and standing on command. This makes him easy to manoeuvre, and to load up. There is nothing more irritating (and potentially dangerous) than loading a horse who won't stand still.

* ideally, is on the smaller rather than the taller side – simply because it's easier to pack a horse if you're not having to reach up on tiptoe.

We used a mare for many years who, due to poor early training with a previous owner, was always a difficult ride, constantly pulling, fussing and jogging. She was however impeccable as a packhorse: calm, obedient and reliable, with lovely manners.

Pack saddles

In the UK, there is less of a tradition of using packhorses (although it is rapidly becoming more popular.) As such, it can sometimes be difficult to find suitable saddles – although they are readily available from the USA and Europe via the internet (you can find some suggestions in Chapter 11 *Further Resources.*)

However, to begin with, you are probably reluctant to spend a fortune on new equipment, so let's look at possible solutions. A traditional English riding saddle is not likely to be suitable, except for the very lightest of loads, as they are not designed to carry dead weight. You are looking for a saddle which will hold a load securely, has secure fastening points for gear (which can if necessary be added by any saddler), and distributes the weight evenly over as large a surface area as possible with minimal slipping or rolling. Naturally, it must also fit the horse, just as well as a riding saddle: particular attention needs to be paid to spine clearance and saddle width, as discussed in Chapter 3 *Equipment.*

Western saddles

We know of quite a few people who use these successfully for packing: unlike most conventional 'English' riding saddles, they are designed with a large weight-bearing surface, are ruggedly built, and usually feature a large selection of D rings for attaching gear safely and securely. On traditionally built Western saddles the bars which form the rigid tree are longer than English saddles, and therefore helpful for distributing the weight of the packs. This sturdy construction does however add extra weight to the saddle. Western saddles are always used in conjunction with a pad or a blanket underneath, as they usually have much less padding than their English counterparts.

They are not always suitable for very short-backed , close coupled animals, as they may extend too far over the loins.

The similar Australian stock saddles which are fairly readily available offer many of the same advantages. However, a word of warning: as they are designed for high-withered, narrow-bodied Australian stock horses, you must make certain that they are wide enough for your horse or pony. The ones we've seen are often on the narrow side for the average British animal. Both Western and Australian saddles may be heavy - in the 20-25 kg range.

Stalking saddles

These are traditionally used for carrying red deer stags off the Scottish mountains during the hunting season. With the advent of quad bikes and tracked vehicles in recent years, ponies are less frequently used for this job, and so it's sometimes possible to pick up a good one secondhand.

These are the ultimate weight-bearing saddle, designed to carry stags weighing up to twenty stone, and are designed with a plethora of D-rings and straps for attaching loads, breastplates, cruppers and breechings. We've used them successfully for many years. They do however have two principal disadvantages: being so robust means that they are very heavy (around 30 kg). This is of course a lot of weight for a horse or pony to carry all day – before you've even loaded the packs or panniers on. It's also a lot of weight for you to lug around as well!
The second possible problem is that they are inevitably designed to fit Highland ponies, which are the breed of choice for stalking. Highlands are in general broad-backed and sturdy, with very little in the way of withers, so these saddles definitely do not fit every horse, and as they are heavy and large they are not suitable for smaller ponies.

Any secondhand stalking saddle which comes on the market should be carefully inspected: not only have these saddles often had a hard working life, in recent years many have spent a lot of time hanging up in barns, resulting in the leather drying out and becoming prone to split or crack – the last thing you need many miles from home. There are several saddlers who specialise in the repair and refurbishment of these saddles (and any saddler will be able to effect minor repairs).

Areas of particular concern are the girth straps and D-rings which should be inspected very carefully – these are the things which tend to break without warning when put under strain. Traditionally they were stuffed with straw and horsehair, and careful inspection will reveal if the stuffing has compacted into lumpy areas, which can sometimes happen and which will make your horse very sore. Make sure the lining (traditionally sturdy cloth) is taut and wrinkle free.

Treeless saddles

We are aware that not every horseman wholeheartedly approves of treeless saddles, whilst others would never use anything else! A quick internet search will reveal a plethora of opinions. Ultimately it comes down to your own judgement and experience.
We have however used *quality* treeless saddles extensively for pack trips lasting weeks or months, with no problems. For the pack horse, they have several advantages:

* they are readily available, even second hand

* in general, they fit a wide range of horses and ponies

* depending on the brand, they are usually lightweight

* many of them have a range of D rings and fastening points for packs and panniers.

* they have a wider, longer seat than treed saddles, helpful for weight distribution

* they can also be used for riding (if you have a friend joining you for the day, for example.)

Most of them require the use of a specialist pad underneath the saddle, designed to aid spine clearance. Beware of suspiciously cheap non-branded saddles (often found on EBay and similar) – they can be very shoddily constructed.

Whichever saddle you use, you will need two additional pieces of equipment: a breastplate and a crupper (or breeching, if the load is heavy and you are crossing mountainous terrain). Unlike a rider, panniers will not compensate for changes in balance going up and down steep hills (or hop off when the going gets rough, for that matter.) The breastplate and crupper are essential to stop the dead weight of the load pushing the saddle backward or forwards on slopes. They will also (to some extent) stop the saddle shifting sideways, or at least give you a breathing space to hop off your riding horse and adjust the load, if a wreck starts to look likely. These should be fitted as explained in Chapter 3 *Equipment*.

You will also need to pay close attention to what type of girth you are using (and its cleanliness) as you will need to girth your horse very snugly to stop the saddle slipping under strain. A traditional method is to use single girths but to cross them under the horse's belly, so that the girth attached to the front girth strap on the near side is attached to the rear girth strap on the off side, and vice versa. If you have a third girth strap on the saddle, a third girth is attached to the middle strap on both sides. This is the last girth to be done up, on top of the other two, and makes for a secure girthing system – provided you check them regularly, tightening them if required.

As with your riding horse, don't expect your packhorse to carry on with a tight girth hour after hour - you'll have problems. Try to take the saddle off (or at the very least, slacken the girths) evry few hours to aid circulation. Remember to tighten them up again before you set off!

Packs and Panniers

The simplest system consists of a pannier either side of the horse, attached to the saddle at several points and usually with an additional belly strap which goes underneath the horse.

This type of arrangement is perfectly serviceable, provided the panniers are carefully packed to be even in bulk and weight, and that nothing which is hard or sharp is packed so that it is in contact with the horse.

You want to have weightier items towards the front of the packs: it's easier for the horse to carry the most weight over the strongest part of his back. You can add a couple of smaller, padded packs at the front of the saddle to carry smaller, heavier items.

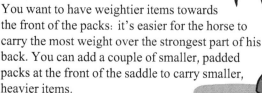

There is a plethora of different designs on the international market: hard and soft bodied, large and small. In the UK, don't discount the possibility of altering packs designed for walkers and cyclists. Many of these are lightweight but made from ultra-strong material. Many people have travelled thousands of miles with a home-designed system, often attached to the saddle with climbing carabiners (quick-release clips, available in outdoor shops.)

As with so much else to do with off-road riding, there is no purist 'right' or 'wrong' (provided the horse is comfortable). What is perfect for one combination may not be for another. Talk to other riders and experiment until you arrive at the system which works for you and your horse.

Pannier Tips

If you're looking at panniers (or thinking of making them), make

sure:

The straps which lay over the saddle are as wide as

possible, to help distribute the weight of the panniers

The clips or fastenings which attach to the D-rings on

the saddle are as robust as possible, but also easy to undo

quickly in an emergency

The panniers are made from tough, rip-resistant material, and all seams are

double stitched. Ideally the side which is next to the horse has some form of

padding.

Unless you're in training for the Ironman Challenge, look for panniers which can be

loaded singly – trying to lift two panniers at once over a horse's back is a bit of a strain

for all concerned – and extremely difficult to do single-handed.

The photographs on page 131 give some examples of packhorses and their gear.

Training the packhorse

Much of the basic training for your packhorse echoes that for the ridden horse, especially standing, moving over, leading and backing up. In addition, your packhorse will benefit from extra attention to the section on ropes (page 87-88) – you absolutely *will* get tangled up or snagged on an obstacle sooner or later, and this shouldn't be a cause for panic.

Time spent getting the horse thoroughly accustomed to the noise of the panniers as they rub against things or drop to the ground is time well spent. Don't expect a horse which has done nothing more than carry panniers around a safe paddock to be reliable out in the countryside. If twiggy branches are whipping against the packs and he's already feeling nervous or excited, he may well boil over.

As usual, thorough preparation at home is the key. For training, you don't need to load him up with all your kit every time: just stuff the panniers with old pillows or similar. The principal thing he has to learn is how wide he now is.

Getting started with your packhorse

The best place to start is with you on the ground, leading him. Before attempting this exercise, he **must** have the basic manoeuvring skills in place (see Chapter 4 - *The Training Starts Here*), and some experience of carrying panniers calmly. He'll then be ready to start practising negotiating obstacles.

For this you will need some jump stands or barrels, with which you can set up a simple little course. Whatever you use should be free of anything sticking out, which could catch on the packs, and if the worst happens and he blunders into them, will just move easily enough to let him through. A lovely assistant is also helpful, should you have one, for moving the jump wings. To begin with, have them wide enough so he can pass through easily even with a bit of wobbling.

Your intention is to teach him to pass through the obstacles calmly and slowly. Every so often, get him to stop between the wings, and back out of the obstacle (a useful skill on the trail when you discover your spatial awareness isn't as good as you thought.)

Once he's managing this happily, make it a little more difficult by moving the jump wings gradually closer together, and repeat the exercise, again with plenty of stopping and backing out. What you're teaching him is that he must listen to your instructions, and not barge through regardless.

As the obstacles get progressively narrower, the packs will start to touch them. He will begin to become accustomed to the noise and feel of this happening, and realise that it's not something to panic about. Please believe us when we say this is time well spent – on the trail the last thing you want is him jumping forward through a narrow gateway in a panic, ripping the packs and strewing your knickers across the landscape.

Once he's got the hang of it, you can practice the same exercises leading him off another horse. It's handy to have your assistant with you at each obstacle to begin with – he/she can help steer the pack animal through if there's any confusion.

When it's all going well with the 'safe' obstacles, you can start practising with more solid obstacles out on a hack: gateways, gaps in stone walls, between trees and similar. You may like to lead him on foot to begin with, where you have closer control over him – the last thing you want to do at this stage is to give him a fright.

Ride and Lead

Classically this is done with the rider leading the horse with her left hand, with the led horse's head at the near side shoulder of the ridden horse. This is so the led horse is away from the traffic when out on the roads.

You are however going to be out for many hours and covering different terrain and because of this you should teach your horses to ride and lead from both sides. This helps to ensure that both you and the horses don't become one sided or unbalanced.

For our purposes, the led horse should also be taught to be a little further away on a longer rope than is traditional. This is because the packs are wide - if the horses are too close they may bump together causing bruising, especially to your lower legs.

You need to be able to ride with your reins in one hand.

 **The photographs on page 138 show recognised ways of riding single handed.**

The led horse should be in a headcollar and long thick lead rope and is led with the free hand. If you need to have him in a bridle to stop him, he's not yet ready – revise his leading practice. You should be wearing gloves (trust us on this one).

We are not fans of leading a packhorse with a bridle on - if he balks or stops suddenly, you can really yank on his mouth. However, you may wish to consider it when you're riding on the road, if you feel you may need extra control. Use a bit coupling for even pressure on the bit (the same as for showing horses in hand.)

To begin with, the led horse need not be saddled. Don't wrap the lead rope round your hand: instead, arrange it in a series of flat loops (like a lunge rein) which you can release a little if necessary.

The training should start with an assistant leading the led horse alongside the ridden horse. Once you've established the horses aren't going to kick or bite each other the rider can start to lead the horse, with the assistant continuing to walk on the other side of the led horse in case of difficulty. Voice aids are a must so that that led horse knows what to do.

If the led horse gets a little too close then a small 'flick' with the rope should be enough to get him to move away along with the verbal command 'over' which he should remember from his ground training. Practice this from both sides.

If he hangs back, give him several quick jerks with the lead rope and growl at him to step up: don't just pull or you may find yourself disappearing off the back of the saddle! The assistant can be useful here too, chasing him forward, with a short sharp smack if necessary. Once he's sped up and is in the right place, praise him.

Once you've all got the hang of it, you will also need to teach him to follow directly behind you, for narrow tracks. You can use a command like ' behind': if you use it every time you put the horse there in time he will recognise the word and know the action.

It all takes practice, as there's quite a lot to think about. Naturally it's all much easier if your ridden animal is obliging about stopping, starting and moving over easily. Most horses enjoy being out together, although some can be quite competitive about whose nose is in front. You need to be disciplined if this is the case, otherwise you may find yourself reaching warp speed rather quickly!

Leading a Packhorse: Safety Tips

Things can go wrong quickly, especially while you're all learning.

NEVER tie a packhorse to your riding horse, saddle or yourself.

NEVER wrap the leadrope around your hand.

Riding on the Road

This is something which riders often feel a little nervous about – with justification. In practice, we have found that drivers on the whole tend to give you more room when you have a packhorse – perhaps you just appear a more solid obstacle. Don't attempt it until you have had plenty of practice in a safe environment – you need to feel confident that you can control both horses in any situation.

The led horse is always between you and the verge: ideally you want his head somewhere near your knee. This means you have close control over his head, and also the pack saddle is not banging into your leg. Use your outside (right) leg just behind the girth to stop your ridden horse's quarters swinging out into the road.

You may not be inclined to give drivers who slow down for you your usual cheerful 'thank you' wave, as your hands are rather full – but a smile and a nod are always appreciated. Personally we always wear reflective safety gear when riding on the road, and feel convinced that drivers are more inclined to slow down when this is the case.

How much can a packhorse carry?

Old military records show packhorses and mules carrying phenomenal loads - up to 180 kg (400 lbs). However, their working lifespan was not great (just a few years) and you are hopefully unlikely to want to carry anything like that.

It is harder for a horse to carry 'dead' weight than to carry a rider: the load will not adjust itself to take account of terrain as a rider naturally would. Received wisdom suggests that a horse can carry about 20% of his bodyweight - so for an avarage 500kg (1100 lb) horse, that's a load of 100 kgs (220 lb).

That's still a lot of gear, and unless you're planning on crossing the Serengeti, you are unlikely to be carrying anything like as much, especially if:

- **you have a young or elderly packhorse**

- **you are covering big daily mileages**

- **you are using anything other than a well–fitting custom packsaddle**

- **you are using a small or lightweight pony**

- **the weather conditions are likely to be extreme (hot or cold)**

- **the terrain is steep or otherwise difficult.**

For your reference, on a recent 1000 mile unsupported hill trip, Kate's packpony carried a maximum of 36 kgs (80 lbs) of gear. This was planned as a particularly lightweight trip and much of the gear was selected on the basis of weight. The recent drive towards 'ultralight' in the walking and climbing world has led to the development of much lightweight equipment.

There are many advantages to keeping the weight down - you may well find (as she did) that you often have to heft the packs about yourself at the beginning or end of the day, or that you have to load and unload on your own (sometimes several times a day) - hard work if the packs are heavy.

On the other hand, you needn't be unneccesarily soft on your packhorse - he's there to do a job after all! For some reason, heavier loads, provided they are well-packed, tend to be more stable, particularly going down steep hills.

The key of course is in the skill of the packing and the distribution of weight: your horse will find it easier to carry a heavier, well-packed load than a lighter, badly packed one.

Distributing the Load

Without knowing your precise set-up (and exactly what you're planning to carry), it's difficult to be specific, although we have assumed you are using some form of pannier system. However, there are some tried and tested 'rules' which apply to any pack outfit. Loading a horse is easier in the beginning with two people; with a little practice (and a compliant horse) you will be able to do it on your own.

Adjusting tack. To begin with, adjust the breastplate, crupper and breeching (if using). Tighten the girths. These are all easier to do before the packs are loaded, although you may need to make further adjustments after the load has settled.

Height of packs (on the horse). In general, you want the packs hitched fairly high (not so high that they make the horse top-heavy or unbalanced, though). They will be easier for the horse to carry than low-slung packs, which will press on his ribcage. It's not so different from you carrying a heavy rucksack: do you find it easier to carry it hitched high up on your back, or dangling somewhere round your hips?

Pack balance. A seriously good investment is a small spring balance scale (of the type fishermen use) on which you can weigh each pack. This will help you get the weight of the packs absolutely equal. Don't underestimate the importance of this: a difference of a very few pounds will ensure you are plagued with a constantly slipping load. Sometimes, despite your best careful efforts, you find there is still some slippage on the trail: a quick temporary solution is to pop a handy rock into the pack which is riding up to balance things out.

Once the horse is loaded, take time to examine him from the front and back to make sure the packs are riding level. Note he's got to be standing square: if he's resting a hind leg, you won't be able to tell how level they are.

Padding. The panniers shouldn't directly touch the horse. If your panniers are wider than the saddle, you'll need an extra large saddle pad. You may also want to consider internal padding for hard and sharp objects: a simple lightweight remedy is an ordinary jiffy bag inside a waterproof bag, such as those made by Exped. Bagging up items also helps tremendously in keeping items separated when you come to unpack at the end of the day: facing all your possessions in a jumbled mess can be somewhat dispiriting!

Belly strap. Panniers should have an additional strap which connects the panniers together underneath the horse to add extra stability, particularly if the horse is trotting or has to hop a downed tree. This should be snugly adjusted, but needn't be as tight as the girth.

General housekeeping. Make sure that all straps are tucked into their keepers, and that you don't have extraneous items dangling off your horse – they will inevitably get jammed on a gatepost or a tree, or flap about annoying both you and your packhorse. A nylon dog collar or a strap off luggage or a rucksack is useful to carry and makes a good spare strap in case of emergency.

Heading Off

Now that the two of you have become three , things are about to get more complicated. As when driving a vehicle with a trailer attached, you will need to learn to think and plan ahead. You need to pay attention – not only to where you're going but also at the load and particularly at the balance of the packsaddle.

Train your eye to spot when it's going off-centre: watch the pommel and the D ring to which the crupper's attached. Once a saddle starts to shift, it WILL continue, eventually ending up under the horse's belly (a 'wreck' in packing parlance). Wrecks are time-consuming and potentially dangerous to unravel, especially on a narrow track on the side of a steep hillside. So, at the first sign of movement, STOP, dismount and readjust. A stitch in time definitely saves nine in this case. Slipping loads cause sore backs and unsettle any horse.

Part of your planning will involve trying to avoid sudden acceleration or deceleration. Slow down in plenty of time approaching stream crossings, bridges, downed trees and the like. Try where possible to keep turns sweeping and gentle, to minimise your horses being thrown off balance.

You already know that you need more room to manoeuvre. Where the track is narrow, for example through a wood, your packhorse needs to follow directly behind your riding horse: close enough that he doesn't go the wrong side of a tree and come to a sudden, jarring halt, but far enough back that he's not treading on the heels of your riding horse. This is a common injury and can bring your journey to an abrupt end, especially if the packhorse is frightened by something behind him and suddenly rushes forward in panic.

Your chances of a wreck are minimised if:

* **the saddle fits well**
* **the crupper and breastplate are properly adjusted**
* **girths are snugly fastened**
* **the loads are well packed and evenly balanced**
* **you pay attention and correct problems as they arise**

It's also helpful if your packhorse has a defined wither and hasn't got a body shape reminiscent of a toilet roll, but you can't always have everything...

Packhorse travelling loose

Herd instinct will generally ensure that even if you let your packhorse loose (obviously not on the road!) he will happily follow you along the track. This may seem rather idyllic in remote areas, and you may have seen very experienced packhorses doing just that. Should you be tempted to give it a try, beware of him:

* **stopping to graze (then cantering to catch up, shifting the load)**

* **taking shortcuts across unsuitable ground or getting stuck in trees or undergrowth**

* **getting sweaty and stopping to roll (particularly tough on your camera or sandwiches)**

* **getting spooked and turning tail for home at speed**

* **frightening other track users. Many walkers or mountain bikers take a dim view of a horse bearing down on them, convinced they're carrying polos!**

If you don't have him beside you and things start to go wrong, you are not in a position to help him – so what could have been a minor blip results instead in an injured or panicking horse.

Using a Packhorse

- A packhorse will increase your self-sufficiency and enable you to carry much more gear. However, it will slow you up and you will require more room to manouevre

- A packhorse should match your ridden horse for pace and the two should get along with one another. You will also have to be able to control him from a distance

- Your packsaddle should fit well, have a good weight-bearing surface with enough fixing points, and be secured with a crupper and breastplate

- Panniers need not be expensive, but they should be well designed and firmly secured

- Both your ridden horse and your packhorse should be trained to cope with ropes and the noise of panniers brushing against things. In addition, your packhorse also needs to learn about manoeuvring through tight spaces

- Be careful about allowing your packhorse to follow along loose

Trying it out – Day and Weekend Trips

8

So at last you're ready to set off ('about time!' we hear you mutter, in a mutinous sort of way). Everything we have covered up till now will be useful to you, sooner or later, but before you go, there's one or two more things you may find handy.

This chapter covers planning your route, finding your way 'out there', and looking after your own safety (and that of others.)

It also tells you how to look after your horse on the trip and after you get back, thus making sure he has as good a time as you do.

Hopefully by now you're itching to have a go! The good news is you can tailor your first rides to your horse's level of training and fitness – you don't need to wait until he's foot perfect in every way before venturing out. He will learn a great deal out there – and so will you.

There is a basic minimum level of training without which it would be foolish to go anywhere. If you cannot answer 'yes' honestly to the following questions, you need to spend more time in a safe enclosed area practising these skills.

Is he ready?

- Will he stand for mounting and dismounting?

- Will he lead politely from both sides, without pulling, hanging back, barging or treading on you?

- Will he go at the pace you ask when ridden?

- Can you stop him?

- Is he obedient in light traffic?

- Is he relaxed with the saddlebags you intend to use, and the gear you are intending to wear? (The middle of a windy hillside in a strange place is not the ideal moment to introduce him to your new fluorescent crackly overtrousers).

- Is he happy if you unfold a map (dismounted to begin with)?

- If the route involves going somewhere in a trailer or lorry, does he load and travel calmly?

If the answer to any of the above is 'no' or 'not always', please spend more time on your training at home, otherwise you are a wreck waiting to happen. If he doesn't do it at home, in familiar surroundings, he won't suddenly do it somewhere strange, when he is excited and/or nervous.

Navigation 101 (or, Not All Wanderers are Lost)

You will enjoy your rides more if you know where you are going (and where you are). Basic navigation skills are not difficult to learn (as well as being quite fun) and there is a list of books and organisations to help you in Chapter 11 *Further Resources.*

You will need a good map – the Ordnance Survey Explorer Series 1:25000 (2 ½ inches to the mile) are excellent, or you could use the smaller scale Ordnance Survey Landranger maps 1:50000 (1 ¼ inches to the mile). These naturally contain less detail than the Explorer Series, but are still useful, and may mean you have to buy one map instead of two. Other companies produce maps for walkers in popular locations (eg Harvey Maps) and these too, are suitable.

It is worth using an up to date map: the Ordnance Survey maps are revised and updated regularly by their mapping intelligence unit. The date of revision is generally shown on the back cover and at the top of the map legend inside (or 'Customer Information' as it is now called!) Up to date maps are increasingly showing access areas, recreational routes etc, which may be of interest to you. A map can only be a snapshot in time, really, as the world around us is constantly changing, but an up-to-date OS map or similar is pretty good.

Other possible options are to use a digital map (Anquet or Memory Map are well-known brands) on short rides. Choose your section of map on computer, print it (and laminate it for weatherproofness) - hey presto, a waterproof map centred on your route. Digital maps come in blocks (about seven cover the UK) - you can buy one block or group of blocks.

These can also be used in conjuction with a GPS (Global Positioning System). GPS has become a widely used aid to navigation worldwide, and can be an extremely useful tool.

Considering GPS?

You can carry a huge variety of maps in the palm of your hand.

The unit will pinpoint exactly where you are on the map.

The electronic compass is easier to use than a traditional compass when you're on the move. The GPS unit will let you know how much distance you've covered and how much further you have to go. It will even tell you your altitude.

A GPS unit runs on batteries which can run out. You can carry extras, but that's extra weight. It's an electronic device –– it can break or stop working if you drop it or if it gets wet. They're expensive, and require a strong signal to work accurately. It may not receive a signal inside buildings or sometimes in forests or valleys.

A GPS unit may provide you with much more detailed navigational information than you could ever get with a compass. But because it relies on battery power and a clear signal, any rider should always have a good old-fashioned compass and a map, as well.

Please do not rely on maps in leaflets or books (they don't show enough detail); road maps (ditto); or the sketch map your friend drew on a napkin at the Riding Club dinner dance. Even if the route is waymarked, the markers have an uncanny habit of disappearing or being turned round by pranksters (or householders who don't like the fact a public bridleway goes past their garden).

Even if you have a good map showing the bridleway or route, you may find that you are not able to follow it all the way - a ford which turns out to be too high to cross, or other obstruction, may mean you have to take a detour. If your map only shows the route and not the surrounding countryside, you are likely to get lost or end up travelling much further than you need to get back on track. A good map will also help you if you have to seek help because of lameness or injury (hopefully you won't need to.)

The basic map skills you will find helpful are:

- **interpreting the map;**

- **calculating distance and height;**

- **'setting the map' using a compass or features you can see;**

- **'ticking off' features as you pass;**

- **being able to give a grid reference.**

Once you have a basic understanding of these concepts, you can be confident of finding your route.

MAPS

Don't be scared!

Many people (and some horses) are frightened of maps. A map tells you (almost) everything - except how to fold it in a high wind. Everything is there for a reason and means something. If you are one of those people (and there are many) who claim they don't 'do' maps, hopefully we can help. A little time spent getting familiar with the map symbols on the right edge of the map is recommended. For more information, visit *www.ordnancesurvey.co.uk* which has lots of hints and tips.

If you're still confused, the best thing is to invest in a day course in basic navigation – lots of outdoor centres, mountain safety organisations and local authorities run them, and they are often subsidised. Bridleways groups, access groups, some branches of the Pony Club, Endurance GB and Scottish Endurance Riding Club also run map-reading courses. There are also recommended books about navigation in Chapter 11 *Further Resources*.

Some horses are frightened of maps

What a map can tell you:

- **The route of paths and tracks (note: this does not necessarily mean you can ride along them; see Chapter 3 *Where to Ride* for further explanation);**
- **where rivers and streams are and how wide they are (sadly, not how deep!)**
- **location of bridges and other crossing points (for rivers, motorways and railways);**
- **how steep the ground is;**
- **Points of interest you might want to see en route;**
- **Points you may wish to avoid: eg busy road junctions, marshland, cliffs etc.**
- **How long your proposed route is.**

As a quick rule of thumb, remember that the map is overlaid already with a grid – the lines are 1km apart. (If you ever paid attention in geometry, though, you will know that if the track goes diagonally across a square, that's not 1 km but 1.4 km). Overall, it's not disastrously inaccurate if all you want is a rough idea.

How long will it take?

It is not always easy to be precise, because 'it depends'. It depends on many different factors: how well your horse copes with the trip; how long you have to spend negotiating difficult gates or other hazards; how much climbing and descending you have to do; how long it takes you to get your horse past those scary pigs you didn't expect; how lost you get; how much time you spend on other things like photography (or lunch).

However, it is possible to make a good estimate. Measure the route on your map using a map wheel or a piece of string. Decide early on if you are going to work in kilometres or miles and stick to that. From the voice of (bitter) experience, we can tell you that 29 miles is a great deal further than 29 kilometres – that's the kind of mistake you only make once! The advantage of working in kilometres, if you can, is that they are easier to count off on the map, because of the overlying grid.

Speed is a personal thing, based on not only what your horse (and you) can physically achieve, but also what you want to do. Do you want to mosey along, admiring the scenery and taking lots of photos? If you take on more than you and your horse are physically or mentally ready for, you increase the risk of injury, get tired and grumpy and generally don't have a good time. Experience will show you what is possible. While you're gaining that experience, be cautious – much better for you both to complete shorter rides successfully and eager for more.

Naismith's Rule

Walkers have long used Naismith's rule, which states that every 3 miles (5km) of distance takes one hour. Then add half an hour for each 1000 ft (300meters) of ascent. So a 12 mile (20km) route which includes 2000 feet (600m) of ascent (you can work out the ascent from the contour lines on the map- see below) should take in the region of 5 hours. This doesn't take into account any breaks.

Naismith's rule works fairly well for horses, too, if you are mostly riding at a swinging walk. Your horse may walk a little faster than a person, but there is generally a bit more fiddling about at gates, mounting and dismounting etc.

If you are including long periods of steady trotting, your speed will naturally increase, probably in the region of 5/6 miles an hour. Experience will tell you quite quickly what is a reasonable pace for your particular horse. Bear in mind that you will not be as fast as you are on familiar routes at home, or on a competitive endurance ride with waymarked routes and stewards to open gates.

Once you have worked out the miles (OR kilometres) and timing, it is good practice to add on another 25% onto your overall time, especially if you are riding at a time

Naismith's Rule

The basic rule is as follows:

Allow 1 hour for every 3 miles (5 km) forward, plus ½ hour for every 1000 feet (300 metres) of ascent. This is equivalent to a horse walking.

When riding in groups, calculate for the speed of the slowest horse.

It does not account for delays, such as breaks for rest or sight-seeing, or for navigational obstacles.

of year when darkness falls early. This 25% can quickly be taken up by snacks, pee stops, watching wildlife, difficult terrain, windy conditions, muddy going or parts of the route where there is no path or track.

How steep is it?

Height is shown by the brown contour lines on the map. Basically, the closer together they are, the steeper the ground. Every fifth contour line is printed in bold. The distance between contours varies: which one your particular map is using will be in the map data. On the Explorer Maps (1:25 000), the contours are usually spaced 5 metres apart on lowland maps, and 10 metres apart on upland ones. A useful tip is to remember that the top of the brown numbers on the contour lines always point uphill, so you can tell whether a slope is going up or down. Remember also that water in rivers or streams always flows downhill!

Rider Tip – Contours

If you're relatively new to map reading, a good trick is to look up a local hill that you know well– that will give you a mental benchmark of steepness. Other hills on the map will have contour lines closer together than 'your' hill (and it will therefore be steeper) or further apart (therefore not as steep).

Setting the Map

Setting the map means holding it so that you can see features in the landscape which correspond with the features on the map. There are two ways to do it: by using features you can see, or by using a compass. When the map is set, what is in front of you on the ground will also be in front of you on the map.

NB: when the map is set, the writing may be upside down – it's the features which are important.

Good features which will help with setting the map are linear features (roads, tracks or rivers), identifiable buildings (church, pub, school).

And Go!

To set the map according to the features, you merely need to rotate the map (and possibly yourself) until the features on the map are arranged as per the landscape in front of you. It is good practice to set the map fairly frequently, so you've always got a good idea where you are. You can also set the map this way if you're lost, provided visibility is good enough for you to be able to pick out identifiable features. This is a little more difficult if you are riding across moorland or hill ground where it all looks more or less the same, or if visibility is poor due to rain, mist or fading light. Then you'll be glad you learned to use a compass.

Using a compass

- Set the compass dial to north. (It will align with the arrow at the top.)

- With the compass on the map, hold it so the long side of the compass baseplate is aligned with the grid lines printed on the map pointing north (that's to the top of the map).

- Holding them both flat out in front of you, rotate yourself around (slowly) until the red end of the compass needle is aligned with the red arrow inside the circle. You've set the map! You will be able to relate features which you see on the ground in front of you (or to the left or right) with features on the map.

However...you will be facing north, which may not be what you want! To set the map quickly, place the compass on the map and turn both compass and map until the end of the needle points to north on the map.

Rider Tip – er, north is north, right?

You'll find it helpful to have a basic understanding of *magnetic variation.*

MAGNETIC NORTH is where your compass needle points (currently somewhere in Canada, moving gently east) and GRID NORTH is the top of the map.

This leads to a variation of about 4°, (the exact amount is shown in the map legend) which can translate to a deviation of about 70 metres per kilometre travelled. Does it matter? It may not, if you're frequently ticking off (see below) – but if you're planning riding in poor visibilty near dangerous cliffs, check out www.http://www.scoutingresources.org.uk/compass/compass_magvar.html for useful instructions!

In the UK, the compass bearing is always greater than the map bearing. To convert from a map bearing to a compass bearing ADD the magnetic variation. To convert from a compass bearing to a map bearing SUBTRACT the magnetic variation. This can be easily remembered using the phrase:

'ADD FOR MAG(netic) – GET RID FOR GRID'

'Ticking Off'

When you're riding, you should check the map fairly frequently, especially when you are changing direction. Much better to know where you are... This is a skill which can (and should) be practised on your own two feet, before you set off.

When you are planning your route on the map, you will be able to identify features that you will pass – a church, a bridge, a forestry plantation. When you actually come to ride the route, by mentally 'ticking off' each feature as you pass, you will be reassured that you are in the right place. It also gives you a firm point to go back to if you get lost.

For an example of how to read a map while 'ticking off', please see pages 132 & 133.

Grid references

Aaargh - numbers! Don't panic - they're easy to learn, and once you know how to find a grid reference, you will be able to:

• give your precise location (eg to the emergency services)

• arrange precisely where to meet your friend with a trailer

• find a hostel or bothy (which often use grid references – there are no street names in the hills).

If you look closely at your map, you will see that it is overlaid with pale blue lines. In the UK, these lines are part of the National Grid: a grid of lines covering the whole country in 100 kilometre squares.

Each 100 km square has two identifying letters: for example, where we live is in grid square NO, which covers the lower half of eastern Scotland. If we look in any of the corners of the map of this area, we will see these letters printed in bold blue outline. On some maps which cross the boundary of a square, the letters which identify the neighbouring square will be printed elsewhere on the map, at the edge of this boundary.

And Go!

OK, so you can identify your position to within a hundred kilometres - which is a start, but not necessarily helpful if you're trying to locate your trailer.

If you look again at your map, you will see a grid overprinted on it. Each square represents a kilometre. Every ten squares, you will see a line of numbers. The horizontal ones are called **eastings**, and the vertical ones are **northings**.

These are the numbers you will use to find a **six-figure grid reference**. Pay attention now, because the emergency services really like these, as they give accuracy to within a hundred metres. If you use a handheld GPS (Global Positioning System), they generally use a 10 figure grid reference, with a claimed accuracy of one metre.

Read the easting number first (ie, read from left to right), then the northing (from bottom to top). The first two easting numbers, followed by the first two northing numbers, will identify which square you (or your target) are in.

Unless the point you want is exactly on a line, you will have to mentally subdivide the square into tenths to give you your last number. For example, if the point you want is exactly in the middle of a square, the last easting digit and the last northing digit will be a 5.

Can Maps Lie?

Erm, not really, at least in the UK, where they are for the most part pretty accurate. This may well not be the case in other countries. However, even in the UK, a 'path' can be anything from a cobbled street to a wither - high bog, and may in fact be impossible to see on the ground.

If you diligently practise the skills outlined above and pay attention, you should pretty well know where you are all the time. The exception is poor visibility - either because it's got dark, or weather conditions have deteriorated so you can no longer see more than a few yards. There are techniques which can help you here, too (although they're outside the scope of this book). See Chapter 10 *Coping With Emergencies* and Chapter 11 *Further Resources* for more help.

Note that *compasses* can lie, or at least give wildly inaccurate readings. This can be due to:

- **Damage to the compass itself (there may be a visible air bubble)**

- **Proximity to metal objects – don't try taking a bearing in a car!**

- **A compass not calibrated for the UK. Any *quality* compass bought in the UK should be fine, that present from Auntie Edna in Australia won't be**

- **Not holding the compass flat so the needle doesn't swing freely**

- **In a few areas of the UK, compasses can be affected by rocks containing magnetite.**

Even with competent map-reading skills, it is of course possible to go off course. If you are practising ticking off features, you should realise your error quite quickly (because features you are expecting to see don't materialise) and be able to retrace your steps.

Our experience suggests you need to pay particular attention leaving large farmyards or other clusters of buildings with tracks leaving from several exits; at junctions where several tracks or paths meet; or when looking for a path which is clearly marked on the map but which may not be so visible on the ground. Flattish moorland areas can be especially challenging, as may be few obvious features. If you're riding along the foot of a narrow glen or valley (or along an old railway which goes through deep cuttings) you're unlikely to get lost, but you may find it difficult to assess exactly how far along the track you are.

A good feature to take account of in this situation is water courses - count them off as you cross them and you'll have a fairly good idea where you are.

Before you set off:

- Have you left your intended route and approximate time of arrival with someone sensible?

- Do you have a map of the area and a compass (and know how to use them?) GPS systems are very handy tools, but may fail if dropped in a river or run out of battery.

- Do you have appropriate clothing, including waterproofs and an extra fleece in case of a change in weather?

- Do you have adequate food (enough for one more meal than you think you'll need)?

- Are you carrying water for yourself or a filtration system (such as a Water Tap – see Further Resources) to enable you to drink safely out of streams?

- Are you carrying a basic first aid kit and do you know how to use it?

- Have you planned your route carefully and timed it (to take account of shorter daylight hours in winter if appropriate)? Have you factored in the possibility of bogs, stony tracks, river crossings, steep hills and gates which may be difficult to open – all of which will slow you down considerably. A torch is essential in winter.

- Are you carrying a whistle and do you know the international distress signal?(Six loud blasts of a whistle, repeated at one–minute intervals). It is far easier and more effective to blow a whistle than to shout for help: the sound carries further, is easier for potential rescuers to locate, and uses less energy if you are ill or injured.

- You may wish to carry a card with some basic information; who you are and where you live and who to contact in the case of an accident. This is a sensible precaution, especially if you have any medical conditions such as epilepsy or diabetes.

- Has your horse been recently shod, and do you have a boot or some other protection if he loses a shoe? Hill tracks can be very stony, eroded or boggy.

Finally – You're Off!

The remainder of this chapter deals with other things which you need to be aware of while you're out enjoying the countryside: how to look after your horse on the ride; and what to do at the end of your journey.

Eating en route

As a general rule, try to stop for 15 minutes grazing (preferably with bit removed) every 1 ½ hours. This is a loose guide: we try never to pass a patch of good grazing as it can be sparse and hard to find especially in the higher hills or when riding through large coniferous forests. As a matter of courtesy, don't help yourself to fields which contain livestock or which are clearly this year's hay crop.

At lunchtime, it's ideal if you can untack your horse(s) and allow them to roll or lie down if they wish. A lightweight electric corral is invaluable for this - the horses can relax, graze or snooze - and so can you. Otherwise, a lightweight lunge line is useful for stopping them heading for home. The only circumstance when we don't untack is if it is raining very heavily, but even then, we remove all packs and panniers, remove bridles to allow them to eat comfortably, and loosen the girths. Wash off the bit before rebridling.

Some riders picket their horses (by a front leg), tether them to a spike (which MUST have a swivel at the headcollar end and the spike end) or hobble them (most usually by hobbling both front legs together). Although these methods of restraint have their uses, we have heard too many tales of horses getting tangled in ropes and panicking or injuring themselves. Hobbled horses can also move surprisingly far, surprisingly quickly - and in difficult ground they may require the use of *all* their legs to keep out of trouble.

Why do horses need to eat so frequently?

The horse's digestive system – unlike ours – is designed to have fibrous food passing through it all the time (grass, hay or chaff and to an extent sugar beet pulp). If the horse does not have fibre moving through his system it can have disastrous results. The bacteria that digest the food die off through starvation. This can be toxic to the horse if it happens in large numbers and can result in complicated colic.

Apart from stopping for grass en route, you may be feeding him sugar beet pulp morning and night. Overnight your horse will need to be corralled in a grassy area or field where he will be able to graze at leisure. If stabled he will need ad–lib hay overnight.

Watering

You need to be sure that your horse doesn't get dehydrated. Don't pass fresh running water without offering your horse a drink. Remember to be patient: if riding in a group, all riders should wait until every horse has had the opportunity to drink - few horses will drink if their companions are disappearing at speed.

Look out for signs of contamination such as bubbly edges. Small puddles may be fresher than larger ponds which may be stagnant.

Be aware of the colour of your horse's urine and how often he has had a pee. If it's becoming darker in colour it might be alerting you to possible dehydration.

Dehydration is when the horse sweats out more water than it has taken in or simply hasn't taken in enough water for normal bodily functions. Dehydration can lead to heatstroke - which can have potentially fatal consequences.

A horse sweating heavily all over can lose up to 5 litres of water through the sweat every hour. Losing as little as 3 litres can cause your horse to start dehydrating, so you need to be aware. You are not likely to be cantering for hours in blistering hot weather (we sincerely hope) but both horse and rider must keep taking in fluids.

Don't forget yourself - dehydration leads to loss of energy and can easily cloud your thinking. It's very easy not to be aware you're getting dehydrated - sip plenty of water as you go.

Testing for dehydration

There are two tests: the *pinch test* and the *capillary re-fill test*.

The pinch test: Pinch the skin on your horse's neck. It should recoil back to being flat immediately. If he is dehydrated it will take longer than two seconds to flatten out.

The capillary re-fill test: Your horse's gums should be salmon pink. If you press hard with your finger, the area will turn white. It should return to salmon pink immediately. Again if this takes longer than 2 seconds to do your horse is dehydrated.

At the end of the day...

- Before you turn your horse out for the night, check all over his body looking for heat, scratches, rubs, abnormal bumps and looking at his general signs of health. Many riders like to wash off the saddle patch and girth area, if this is feasible – it's easier to spot lumps or ticks in wet fur.

- Check the state of his shoes and feet, particularly for loose and twisted shoes or big chunks of horn crumbling.

- Your horse physio may have given you post – exercise rubs to do, and this is the perfect moment.

- Check for signs of dehydration.

- Give the horse his evening feed of sugar beet pulp.

- Leave in peace!

- When you turn your horse loose watch him walk away. He's bound to look a little tired but is he walking with a sound gait? Hopefully you will see him have a drink and perhaps a roll. One or two rolls would be nothing to worry about but if he is continually getting up and down it could be the early signs of colic.

- If your horse is to be stabled overnight, it's good to let him out (on a lunge rein if necessary) to graze a little, roll and urinate if he wants to.

Things to do when you get home

On your return home you still need to be aware of those signs of health. In particular check all over the body for lumps, bumps, rubs and heat. Your horse will appreciate being allowed to graze with his friends and have a little bit of peace.

In the following days keep an eye out for stiffness, which may take a day or two to appear. It's a good idea to take him out for a walk - in hand is fine if your bottom is feeling sore!

Turnout is essential as this is the most natural thing a horse can do. Getting his head down to graze is good for his mental health as well as physically: it will stretch out any (understandably) tired back muscles and he will roam around easing any stiffness.

Ensure he has access to a vitamin and mineral block and don't suddenly cut out the sugar beet - tail it off gradually over a few days if it suits your management regime to stop feeding it altogether.

Trying it Out -
Day & Weekend Trips

- Is your horse ready for an outing? See the checklist on page 181 if you're not sure

- Being able to carry out simple navigation is essential. If you haven't done this before, learn how and practise before you set off

- When planning your route, remember to include factors which may slow you down considerably - terrain, water crossings, lots of gates

- Are you prepared? See 'Before you set off' on page 192

- Careful management of your horse both during and after the ride will ensure you both have a good time - he's not a vehicle! Be prepared to get off and walk at intervals to give him a break

Further &
Higher -
including
Camping

9

Once you and your horse have several day and weekend trips under your belt, you may well feel spurred on to try a multi-day trip, perhaps in somewhat wilder country. One of the things which attracts so many people to off-road riding is the prospect of making 'a journey' — following old drove roads or in the hoofprints of Queen Victoria or Dick Turpin, or riding from one side of the country to the other.

All the training and preparation you've done up till now will stand you in very good stead. This chapter deals with some of the additional things you'll have to think about for longer, more arduous trips, including additional equipment, camping out with your horse, crossing rivers and boggy ground safely, and riding alone. You may find that in order to get tracks to join up you have to ride across open country, or cross a major road or railway, or you may have to ride through the edge of a town.

In this chapter we have collected the information which from experience we believe you'll find helpful — although undoubtedly as time goes on you will gather many additional experiences of your own!

Riding High

Many off-road riders agree that once you've ridden in the mountains, no other landscape ever quite compares, however pretty it may be. The combination of the spectacular views, the solitude and peace, and the sense of achievement from having negotiated obstacles safely is a heady one. However, before you set off to scamper across the slopes like Heidi, there are a few points to consider. If you are a hillwalker or climber, much of this may be familiar to you (although up till now you may not have looked at it from the point of view of a horse!) There is a wealth of information aimed at hillwalkers, climbers and mountain bikers which you too can take advantage of. There are also things you have to consider which they don't (for example, where to find suitable grazing for your horse and how to get across a cattlegrid when there isn't a gate - as well as deer fences, stiles, locked gates and kissing gates.

Terrain

It may sound like stating the (very) obvious but riding in mountainous areas (often referred to, somewhat confusingly, as 'hill ground' or 'the hill' in Scotland) is that there are going to be plenty of steep slopes to negotiate. A friend of ours who trained her horse for a cross-mountain ride in Wales round the pancake-flat lanes of East Anglia found that her lovely gelding really struggled when faced with all those cwms and valleys – he just wasn't physically or mentally ready for that terrain. On the other hand, fit horses used to hunting in an area like the Cheviot Valleys would find much of the UK's upland country a breeze.

What follows are some pointers to consider when planning your route. These are absolutely not meant to scare you to death or put you off, but to help you in your planning process. In particular, they may aid you in estimating what is a reasonable distance for your horse to travel in a day, and how long that may be likely to take.

Hopefully you'll thank us when you bounce in to your overnight stop, with plenty of time to set up camp, cook a delicious dinner and enjoy relaxing watching the sun go down over a well-earned glass of red! If on the other hand you find yourself leading a tired and grumpy horse and trying to get off an unfamiliar mountain in the dark (probably soaked to the skin to boot), eating handfuls of muesli to keep yourself going and thinking murderous thoughts about your so-called friend who planned this so-called fun expedition... well, we've been there too, and promise that the first scenario is much more pleasant. So...

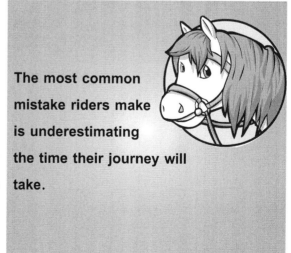

The most common mistake riders make is underestimating the time their journey will take.

Riding High – Points to Consider

- **How fit is your horse?** Going up and down long steep slopes asks a lot of a horse's heart, lungs and muscles. It can take four times as long as covering the equivalent mileage on flat or gently rolling ground, and even longer if the footing is poor. You too will need to be fitter, so that you can hop off and walk with him, often for extended periods. An exhausted horse is no fun to ride (or even lead), and is far more prone to injury and accidents.

- **What is the condition of the track?** Tracks which are in safe well-maintained condition as you leave the farmyard have a nasty habit of deteriorating rapidly the higher you get, becoming boggy, bouldery or transforming themselves into a squishy footpath (that's if they don't disappear altogether.) Infrequent use, or damage from last winter's floods, can render them passable only with great care.

- **Take advice** – from those who know the ground: rangers, landowners, walkers, shepherds or gamekeepers. They are absolutely invaluable on giving you an up to date report of the conditions. Just because someone you know rode through there three years ago doesn't necessarily mean you won't have problems: there may have been landslips, washouts, or bridges destroyed since then.

Bear in mind that other land users may not really have experience of horses or understand their particular needs. 'You'll get across there no bother' may not actually be the case: ground which is easy to pass on foot, or even on a quad bike, may be very hard work for a horse. Don't forget that unlike people or quads, horses have a very large weight concentrated on a very small area (their hooves), which makes crossing soft ground or rotting bridges pretty perilous.

A useful rule of thumb in Scotland...

Tracks marked with a double dashed line usually (not always) are well-surfaced and easily followed without causing damage (although you may still meet locked gates).

Paths marked with a single dash (or which stop and vanish on the map) are often less passable with a horse and need more research if you want to be sure you will get safely through.

Other land users also sometimes forget to mention obstacles such as cattlegrids (because they just don't have to think about them the way we do). The Ordnance Survey 1:25,000 Explorer Series usually have cattlegrids marked, so you can ask about getting round them. There is usually (although not inevitably) a gate beside them, but sometimes it seems as though these haven't been opened since the dawn of time, so they can be great time robbers as you have to hack down vegetation and unravel a veritable macramé of baler twine and wire.

Cattlegrids

If, in spite of your careful efforts, you find yourself stuck at a cattlegrid, you will have to explore the alternatives. In the past, we have got through by

- backtracking a bit and going through fields avoiding the obstacle by taking a slightly different route;

- dismantling sections of post and rail, stepping through, and putting them back together (er, not newly and expensively erected ones, just ones which are on the point of collapse anyway. Leave everything as stockproof as you found it)

- arranging with a farmer to lay **heavy duty, wide** boards across the cattlegrid and leading our horses across.

Yes, we do know people who have jumped them – but a very quick way to a broken leg if things go wrong. Bear in mind that some horses who haven't met cattlegrids before don't appear to immediately understand that they shouldn't just walk over them – so have your wits about you to stop your horse if he looks like doing just that. Take extra care negotiating gates next to cattlegrids (particularly if the cattlegrid appears to be filled in).

Gates

Much of what applies to cattlegrids also applies to gates (particularly in Scotland. In England & Wales, if the track is obstructed and you have a legal right to ride along it, you have every right to remove obstacles - but please repair it afterwards and report the obstruction to the relevant access authority). Naturally, we don't approve of any gates across tracks being locked – but sadly they sometimes are. The purpose of locking gates is very often not to keep *you* out , but to restrain four wheel drive vehicles laden with poachers, or by frustrated farmers sick and tired of gates being left open and their stock escaping. Hopefully your discussions with someone on the ground have resulted in any offending gates being unlocked for you or the loan of a key – but what do you do if you come across one you didn't expect? You may be several miles away from habitation.

The first thing to do is examine the lock carefully. Occasionally the lock is there 'for show' and you will find that there is a loose link in the chain which you can just unhook. It is also worth looking carefully around the gateposts or under nearby stones to see if there is a key secreted away – this is common practice where a number of different vehicles use the track. *(Be certain to put it back exactly where you found it.)*

Another option is to see if you can lift the gate off its hinges and swing that end open to get through, before replacing the gate on its hinges. Be careful – large gates can be pretty heavy and awkward to lift, and suddenly fall over when they are released from their hinges. Ideally, you have a companion who can hold the horses while you struggle – or better still, offer to hold the horses while *she* does it... If all else fails, you will have to look for an alternative route past the obstruction, as for cattlegrids above.

Sometimes you will come across narrow gates which have been put in for pedestrian or cyclist use. If they're not actually 'kissing gate' style, you may be able to get your horse through, although you may have to be prepared to untack him first – a time-consuming but safer option where the gate is narrow. Even hunt gates (designed to be opened from horseback) may be quite narrow – if you're riding your horse through them, you can 'hook' your legs over the front of the saddle flaps to save getting your legs bruised or your feet caught. Be careful though, if your horse moves suddenly your balance is compromised – be prepared to grab the breastplate or a handful of mane.

Hopefully this hasn't put you off! In practice, promoted riding routes and bridleways are very unlikely to have obstructions (but it *can* happen). Again, please report any problems to the local access authority and urge them to take action. The more complaints received, the better!

Weather

You left your campsite at the bottom of the valley in brilliant sunshine, wearing just a T shirt. (Well, hopefully not just a T shirt, but you know what we mean...) You've been riding steadily uphill all morning and are now starting to feel really cold. To add to your woes, it looks as though it's about to start raining... welcome to mountain weather!

Temperature usually falls the higher you go – this is known as the 'lapse rate'. The lapse rate varies according to local conditions, including wind speed and humidity, but an average is about 2 degrees for every 300 metres climbed. In Scotland at least, this effect is referred to as 'a jaiket caulder' [a jacket colder] – meaning you need an extra layer of clothing!

You are also more likely to experience cloud and rain at higher elevations: because air is forced to rise clouds are more likely to form, with the threat of rain – mountains tend to be wetter places than the surrounding valleys. In addition, mountains are on the whole windier too - sometimes very much so. A combination of air temperature and wind speed is referred to as wind chill and can make a serious difference - a 30 mph wind when the air temperature is $0°$ can make it feel as low as $-11°$.

What Should I Do?

Ideally, don't set out without having checked the weather forecast – see information panel on next page. Bear in mind that mountain weather can be very localised: a general weather forecast for the area will give you some idea, but for details you will need to consult a forecast specifically for the mountains.

As well as a forecast, you should make sure you are well-equipped with additional clothing and waterproof jacket/trousers.

Consider the likely visibility - don't set off if the hills are shrouded in mist and you are not a confident map reader. Take extra care to 'tick off' where you are, and stick to tracks which are marked on the map. Now is *not* the time to experiment with crossing open country!

Mountain Weather Information Service (www.mwis.org.uk) Accessible via your mobile phone.

The Met Office (www.metoffice.gov.uk/loutdoor/mountainsafety) issue twice daily forecasts for mountain areas, cover daylight hours and cover hazard risk, overview, 3 hourly weather summary, probability of precipitation, visibility, hill fog, windspeed and general outlook for the next few days. They can also be contacted by telephone (24 hour service) Tel: 0870 900 0100 or 01392 885680

www.metcheck.com – a comprehensive weather service up to 7 days ahead.

TV and Radio. Local radio stations offer detailed weather forecasts, nationally you can also tune into Countryfile or Landward 5 day forecast (11.30 Sundays.) **Daily** 07.55 forecast on BBC Radio Scotland; 18.20 Grampian TV; 18.50 BBC1 national weather ; 19.10 Radio Scotland forecast for hill walkers

Camping

Camping with your horse is immense fun – there is nothing to equal time spent outdoors with your beloved horse companion. You can drift off to sleep listening to his contented munching and wake up together to share the delights of a beautiful summer's morning.

On the other hand, you can spend long dark hours in the rain searching for an escapee, or listening to him pacing up and down being driven mad by midges. As with most things to do with horses, sound preparation is your key to a successful camping trip.

Rider's Tip – Camping

It's common sense, but introduce your horse to tents and corrals

***before* you leave home – you don't want him fleeing for the hills as**

you unpack your 'dragon' tent!

Wild camping

Scotland

In Scotland, access rights include informal camping or 'wild camping' when exercised responsibly. The aim of the legislation is to enable the public to enjoy the outdoors responsibly and experience the open spaces and wild places on their doorstep.

Wild camping is lightweight, done in small numbers and only for a maximum of two or three nights in any one place. You can camp in this way wherever access rights apply but help to avoid causing problems for local people and land managers by not camping in enclosed fields of crops or farm animals and by keeping well away from buildings, roads or historic structures. Take extra care to avoid disturbing deer stalking or grouse shooting. If you wish to camp close to a house or building, seek the owner's permission.

Scottish Natural Heritage

England and Wales

The situation is different in England and Wales – according to the strict letter of the law permission must be obtained prior to pitching a tent and camping.

In practice however, this isn't always practical and wild camping is *sometimes* tolerated in the more remote areas – typically, more than half a day's ride from an official campsite or other accommodation, providing you act responsibly (see below). However, we wouldn't camp anywhere with horses without permission, except in an emergency.

(NB There appears to be an exception to this with respect to camping in Dartmoor National Park where the right to wild camping is actually enshrined in the National Parks & Access to the Countryside Act, 1949 amendment Dartmoor Commons Act, 1985).

Selecting a campsite

Unless it's an emergency, we prefer to have the landowner's permission to camp with our horses if it's at all practicable. Technically if you are on open ground you are 'wild camping' (see box) and in Scotland at least you don't require permission. However, in the interests of landowner/rider relations it is much better if you ask. It's also preferable for your safety: tonight may be the night when vermin shooting is taking place, for example. There's also nothing worse than setting up a camp, snuggling into your sleeping bag, and then being moved on for some reason.

This is a matter of personal choice, but we always offer to pay, as a gesture of goodwill. It's rarely accepted (unless the landowner makes their living from liveries or Horses Welcome). A good relationship with the landowner can benefit you hugely – we have often been offered a bath, breakfast, a barn to dry out our gear or been invited in for a drink and a chat.

The perfect campsite

Finding the perfect campsite means juggling the needs of your horse(s) with your own, as well as taking account of local weather conditions. From the horse's point of view, he would like:

Good quality grazing (and plenty of it – he's worked hard!)

A breezy spot if insects are likely to be a problem in the evening or early morning

But – protection from the wind if it is strong or cold

A sheltered dry spot to lie down

Access to water

No poisonous plants (see box, next page)

No old farm machinery, rolls of wire lying in the grass or other hazards

Avoid corralling on damp ground: several horses can make a lot of mess in confined areas.

Do not camp in a field without permission. Unless you have permission to camp in a safe field, you will have to corral him (see page 185).

Your needs are not too different from his (although you've probably brought your own grazing). You will want to pitch your tent close enough to the corral so you can keep an eye on things, but not too close if you want a decent night's kip – horses can be quite noisy creatures during the night, stamping, munching and -er- farting.

Poisonous plants

In general, horses have good dietary wisdom and tend to avoid poisonous plants. For his safety and your peace of mind, however, learn to identify the following common poisonous plants:

• **Ragwort** • **Oak leaves and acorns (when green)** • **Yew** • **Foxglove** • **Horse or mares tail** • **Bracken (large amounts)** • **Buttercup** • **Hemlock** • **Nightshade** • **St Johns Wort** • **Water Dropwort**

Watch out, too, for other toxic hazards such as dumped potatoes or grain, old silage or abandoned batteries.

A good place to pitch your tent is:

On level ground, free of stones, tree roots and other detritus.

On a well–drained site – not in a hollow in the ground. If it rains in the night you don't want the water collecting under your tent

Not directly beneath a tree (limbs can fall off without warning). Rain will also drip from trees long after a storm has passed

Reasonably near to water (for cooking, washing and watering your horse) but not right next to it (river levels can rise suddenly and flood your tent). In addition, camping next to running water can be very noisy and you may not hear a companion shout (or your horses escaping.)

Restraining your horse

By far the best method of restraining your horse overnight is to use a lightweight electric corral. These are easy to carry, weighing about 2.5 kg and quick to put up if you use folding poles and a lightweight energiser. These run off torch batteries but still carry a hefty sting. We use 10mm electric tape because our horses are well accustomed to being corralled – otherwise you will find 20mm tape is more visible to them. Normally we carry in the region of 200 metres (wound on a lightweight plastic reel) which gives you a large enough area for several horses overnight. You can make your corral larger by using an existing safe fence for one side of the corral.

Even in a well-fenced field, you may find a corral useful for restricting the grazing area (if the field is knee-deep in lush grass); taping off unsafe areas or dodgy looking fencing; or setting up a corral so that you can camp inside in peace, without nosey horses trying to eat your supper or climb into your tent.

If you don't use electric fencing at home, you will have to accustom your horse to it before you leave (see box). Do not assume that horses which don't know each other will get along in a corral (even if you've been riding alongside each other all day). You may have to be prepared to separate them into smaller corrals to avoid bullying or accidents.

Putting up a corral

The sequence of photos on page 140 show how to put up a corral.

If you haven't done it before, it may look complicated and time-consuming, but in reality takes between 5 and 10 minutes.

Accustoming your horse to electric fencing:

Introducing electric fencing needs to be done carefully and your own safety is paramount. This is why you should never try and lead a horse to an electric fence as his reaction may be one of extreme fright, causing him to turn and run.

The best way to go about it is to set up your electric fence and turn your horse out into the area. Watch him for a few minutes – horses often explore their boundaries touching the fence and the job is done for you.

REMEMBER not to stand anywhere near your horse, in case he whips round sharply. If he hasn't been inquisitive and is just scoffing grass you will need to entice him closer.

Try walking around the outside of the fence with a bucket of food rattling to encourage him over to you. Once your horse has touched the fence and got a shock your job is done – he is very unlikely to make the same mistake again!

You will need:

Lightweight folding poles with keepers for the tape

An energiser with batteries

Electric tape

Small rubber bungees

Tent pegs

An electric fence tester is handy if you're not hardy enough to touch the fence to see if it's on!

(See Chapter 11 *Further Resources* for stockists)

Whilst the corral is self-supporting, you can use an existing post or tree at the corners for additional stability. However, you must make sure the electric tape doesn't touch it as this will ground the charge and stop the fence from being live.

- Set up your corners first. While the corral doesn't need to be square, tightly angled corners may result in a horse being trapped by another.

- Either:
   a) set up the corner poles. The folding poles should be unfolded and poked into the ground, and then tensioned with bungees hooked round tent pegs

or

   b) use bungees round existing wooden posts or trees to support the tape at each corner.

- Unwind the tape and feed it through the keepers at each post. The tape should be taut, but not strained to breaking point. If you haven't used all the tape and there's still some on the reel, feed a bungee through the centre hole of the reel and attach it safely to a post or tree – again making sure that the tape isn't touching anything.

- Put up the remainder of the poles, paying particular attention to any odd slopes in the ground – you don't want your horses limbo–dancing underneath the fence.

- Once you are satisfied with the corral, walk round the tape, making sure that any high vegetation is tramped down. Plants touching the tape may also cause it to earth, particularly if they are damp.

- Attach the energiser to the fence. Most models have two leads – a red one which you clip to the fence, and a green one which you attach to the bottom of one of the metal poles. The energiser itself can just be clipped or tied to a pole.

- Switch the energiser on and test the fence – either with a fence tester (our preferred method!) or by touching it with your hand. Most energiser models emit a high–pitched intermittent bleep while they are on – this tells you that the battery power is sufficient.

Note: people who have pacemakers fitted or known heart abnormalities should never touch electric fencing.

Camping equipment

Unlike fellow campers with cars who have the luxury of transporting everything including the kitchen sink with them, we have to consider weight at every turn. As stated earlier, camping with horses is more difficult if you don't have a packhorse. It is feasible - people do it - but it's asking a lot of any horse to carry you *and* all your camping gear, and you will have to be prepared to keep gear weight to an absolute minimum and to get off and walk a lot. An alternative is to get a friend or partner with a vehicle to meet you at a pre-arranged camping spot - in which case you can pack what you like.

The tendency for all riders when setting off is to take way too much, in the hope that 'it will be useful'. On a longer trip, it becomes painful to continually pack and unpack excess stuff - you soon find out what is really necessary.

What follows is a list of what we take for multi-day trips which you can use as a guide. It should give you a good idea of where to start.

You may have different priorities - for example, we don't find clean clothes every day are necessary - you might. For us, though, inflatable sleeping pads are a must - you might be tougher. We carry very little horse food, as we have 'good doers': just enough to disguise some bute should it be necessary. (An experienced off-roading friend of ours find jam sandwiches work just as well for this purpose!)

And Go!

Horses:
Saddle and packsaddle
Saddlepads
Bridle
Breastplate
Crupper (pack horse)
Halters (with ID tags)
Long lead ropes
Electric corral
Quick soak sugar beet
Various packs/ saddlebags
Exped waterproof bag liners
Old Mac Hoof boots
Fly/midge masks

Camping
Tent (Vango Spirit, 2.5 kg)
Sleeping bag and inflatable sleeping pad
Tarpaulin (to keep gear dry overnight)
Trangia meths stove (simple and safe)
Cooking equipment
Waterproof matches
Food
Insect repellent

Personal
Spare clothes, especially SOCKS!
Helmet
Waterproofs
Washing gear
Gloves
Torch
Mobile phone
Wet wipes
Vaseline (you'll find out)
Notebook and pen
Maps and compass

Miscellaneous
Duct tape (fixes anything!)
Wire cutters
Small folding saw
Penknife
Strong string(for tying up and other things)
Bin liners (many uses)

Emergency
Whistle
First aid kit (human/horse)
Space blanket

Camp Routines

You'll find camping a whole lot more pleasurable if you have strict routines. It helps to know where everything is (colour coded drybags are helpful for this) and to deal with things in a strict order. This saves having things strewn about getting wet or damaged. If there is a group of you, each person can take responsibility for certain tasks, saving time (and temper, if you're all feeling tired and sore at the end of the day).

Horses first!
* Unload and untack the horse(s)
* Check for injuries, quick groom, check feet and shoes
* Offer horses water, then feed them (if you do)
* While the horses are eating, put up corral (if necessary). Turn horses out.
* Wash off bits, remove mud from tack, hang numnahs up to air & dry

With the horses safely contained and happily grazing, you can then:
* Put up tent
* Inflate sleeping mats and unroll sleeping bags

210

- Stow your gear – in the tent if it's big enough and you don't mind the smell, or under a small lightweight tarpaulin, or in a nearby barn or shed (if you're lucky).
- Prepare your food. We like to have a quick snack (to get blood sugar levels up), then set about preparing supper. While it's cooking, you can have a wash, change into dry clothes if necessary, do any tack repairs etc.
- Eat, wash up, relax!

Before bed:

- Check horses. Offer them water if they don't have any in their field/corral. You can either lead them to a stream, or take water to them (we use a large waterproof drybag for this, turned inside out.)

The procedure is reversed in the morning : it's usually best to leave the corral up until last to keep the horses contained if you don't have somewhere suitable to tie them up.

Leave No Trace Camping

Your aim should always be to leave your campsite looking as pristine as you (hopefully) found it.

- Keep groups small
- Keep horses out of the 'living area'
- Camp as unobtrusively as possible (that includes excessive noise)
- Do not light fires (except in an emergency) – use your stove for cooking
- Do not cut living trees or shrubs
- Remove all litter (even other people's)
- Carry out everything you carried in
- Carry out tampons and sanitary towels (burying them doesn't work – animals dig them up)
- Choose a dry pitch rather than digging drainage ditches around a tent or moving boulders
- Toilet duties should be performed 30m (100ft) from water and the results buried using a trowel. Use only unscented toilet paper (preferably biodegradable) and bury that with the waste.
- Tie horses to trees only when there is no other option and for short durations
- When ready to leave, check! Have you got everything? Is the site tidy and clean? We spend a few moments scattering piles of dung the horses have left behind – it disappears quicker that way.
- At all times, treat the environment with respect – keeping it both more enjoyable to visit, and ensuring that we are welcome in the future.

- If you are in any doubt about what you're doing, find out more !

211

RIVER CROSSINGS

In a cool temperate climate such as the UK, you generally don't have to go very far off-road before you have to cross water. This may be nothing more than a stream trickling over the track, or it may be a more substantial river or ford. In Chapter 4, we looked at training your horse to cross water, and it is important to practise this at home first.

Rider's Tip – Water Crossings

If your planned route requires a river crossing, study weather reports and the forecast carefully before setting off . Has there been recent heavy rain in the catchment of the river, or is rain forecast?

Where to cross

If at all possible, try to cross at an established ford. While you will still need to take care, in general the footing is better, without hidden deep holes or other hazards. There's a reason why it's where it is!

If you are not crossing at a ford used by vehicles or horses, you will need to investigate your options.

To cross or not – our personal view

We **will** cross:
- fast flowing water: if less than fetlock deep and we can see the bottom
- moderately fast flowing water : if less than knee–deep and we can see the bottom
- slowly flowing water: if less than belly deep

We **won't** cross:
- if the water is deeper than the smallest horse's belly
- if it is very fast flowing, white water
- if there are submerged, sharp, or slippery rocks, or a very uneven bottom
- if there is very deep mud
- if there are deep holes (often found where there are rock 'shelves' close to the bank
- if branches or other detritus are coming down the river
- where the banks at entrance and exit points are undercut and may give way.

Check and check again

Note that you will have to examine the river carefully – a casual inspection may not show up all these dangers. It is preferable if possible to climb to slightly higher ground where you can get a good view of the river. Take the time to thoroughly investigate well above and below where you want to cross. Make certain there are no waterfalls or rapids below your crossing point, in case you get into trouble. Select a point on the opposite bank where you will exit the water. Don't forget to check out your map too. Sometimes it's easier to cross where a large river braids into several smaller ones.

How to cross

Once you've made up your mind where you're going to cross, it's best to ride right up to the crossing without hesitating. Don't make it seem like a big deal. However, lots of horses do like to stop and check things out, so let him lower his head and sniff or drink the water if he wants to. Don't let him start pawing or splashing though – this can be a precursor to getting down for a roll.

If he seems tense, you can let him stand and chill out for a minute or two – don't let him turn away from the crossing though. There's only one way to go! Urge him on with your legs, while talking to him in a reassuring, calm tone of voice. Many riders like to have their feet out of the stirrups at more challenging water crossings, in case the horse stumbles and goes down.

Cross the water at a purposeful walk, without rushing. Where the river bottom is soft, you may find yourself sinking in if you stand still, so try to keep moving. Don't look down at the water (it makes some riders dizzy) – instead, focus on your exit point on the far bank.

General points – water crossings

If crossing in a group, have the most experienced horse/rider combinations at the front and rear of the group, where they can assist other members.

If you decide to lead your horse across, rather than ride him, wear your boots. (You can take your socks off to keep them dry). Otherwise, you run the risk of injuring your feet on sharp rocks, slipping or getting trodden on (ow!)

Walk upstream of him, holding onto his mane or using a strong stick for stability. If you are downstream of him and he loses his footing, you risk being knocked over.

Dry off your feet as much as possible before putting your socks back on. Make sure that all members of the party are warm and dry before setting off along the track. A mishap during a river crossing usually drains your strength. It is usually best to stop and make a hot drink, change into dry clothes, and possibly camp early.

Crossing a river can be a dangerous undertaking. If it looks unsafe, there are always options – see Chapter 10 *Coping with Emergencies.*

BOGGY GROUND

This is one of the most potentially dangerous hazards which you can encounter. Every year, horses get stuck in bogs, and in a few cases panicking horses have broken legs and have had to be humanely destroyed. Not for nothing do old moor men refer to deep bogs as 'stables': ponies are kept in stables and any pony walking into a bog won't be leaving any time soon.

On horseback, **give boggy ground a wide berth if you can.** The difficulty for horses is that they cannot spread their weight and it is all concentrated on their hooves: it is very much harder for a horse or pony to cross boggy ground than a person.

Every off-road rider has had a fright in boggy ground when their horse or pony has got stuck. The vast majority of times, animals get themselves out with some calm encouragement.

What is a bog?

In most weather conditions bar the very driest of summers bogs are permanently waterlogged. They can occur anywhere, but in general they occur on flat or gently sloping ground (more steeply sloping ground naturally tends to be better drained.)

They are often found close to the edges of lakes or lochs, near slow-moving streams and rivers, in the bottom of valleys, and often on the flat tops of hills and mountains in areas of high moorland. They can also occur in wet woodland. Broadly speaking, there are more bogs in the west of the country than in the drier east.

Be aware that bog habitats are very fragile, and in many areas they are designated Sites of Special Scientific Interest because of the flora and fauna they contain. Hooves can do considerable damage, particularly when travelling at speed, so proceed carefully.

Areas of bog or marsh are often identified as such on maps, but it's generally not that precise and tends not to show the exact extent. Sometimes place names give a clue – be alert for words in place names such as mire, mere, moss, carse, dub, flow, quaw, sink, slag, syke, laigh, latch, monadh, moine, howe, hag, fheithe.

Identifying boggy ground

The colour and the vegetation are good clues. Watch out for:

- areas of bright green sphagnum moss
- deergrass
- rushes
- cotton grass, with its distinctive nodding 'cottonwool' seedheads in summer
- clumps of willow trees which thrive in wet areas.

What should I do?

- Proceed **at a walk**. Going any faster means that the horse may already be well into a bog before he can stop. In very boggy terrain, it is safer to dismount and lead him, with the horse following behind you at a safe distance on a long leadrope – not right on your heels.

- Always stick to the track, if there is one. Even if it looks horribly deep and muddy, old hill tracks often have stone or rock bottoming, laid down over many years by hill farmers and stalkers. Accidents occur when riders try to pick their way round the mud and step onto ground which doesn't have any firm bottom.

- When leading your horse, you can use a stick or tent pole to test how deep the bog is.

- Native ponies or native crosses often (although not always) have good 'bog sense' and will refuse to cross ground which they consider dangerous – be certain that it is safe before urging them on. We have animals which will spend some time standing with their muzzles at ground level, before deciding whether or not to proceed. They never seem to get it wrong, (whereas their owners sometimes do.)

- If you land in an area with no track, pick your way along the side of slopes rather than crossing flat areas, which are likely to be much wetter. Alternatively, you can walk along a stream or river bed which may be safer (obviously not if there is a large volume of water coming down it) – look out for hidden holes, branches, large boulders and other hazards.

Bogs – if the worst happens

- Get off your horse, if you haven't already. The last thing he needs is your weight to cope with as well. If possible make sure the horse has a head collar on with a long lead rope but DO NOT place yourself in danger trying to put one on.

- Consider your own safety. If you get stuck as well, how can you help him? Get yourself onto firmer drier ground. Spread your own weight by crawling, if you need to.

- You cannot physically haul a horse out of a bog yourself – your main task is to keep him calm and reassure him while he works out what to do. Many horses will remain stock still while they're thinking about it. If you can, move another calm horse on to dry ground in front of him, so he can see that it is safe.

- Be aware that your horse may suddenly lurch or leap out of the bog towards you. Be prepared to move yourself out of the way quickly. Do not kneel down or squat in front of him. Always approach him from the spinal side – ie away from potentially thrashing legs and feet.

- Do not SHOUT or make loud noises and try to keep everyone around you quiet – noise stimulates a trapped animal causing him to struggle more and potentially injure himself.

- Try and encourage him to get at least his front legs and chest onto firmer ground. You may be able to improve the footing using stones from a nearby wall. He will then be safe, even if it takes him a little while to haul the rest of himself out. Your horse is unlikely to drown – however, in extreme conditions he may require emergency assistance to get him out. (See Chapter 11 *Coping with Emergencies* for how to contact emergency services.)

A horse in a bog is rarely in immediate danger as long as he is kept calm – so don't panic . When professional assistance arrives be prepared to let them do their job and DO NOT interfere with the rescue or try to help unless specifically asked to do so by the person in charge. A horse that has been in a bog may be in shock, be very cold and tired, and will certainly be absolutely filthy. Lead him slowly to somewhere suitable to wash him down and check for injuries, before seeking veterinary help if necessary.

RIDING IN A GROUP

Riding in a group can be very enjoyable. There are many benefits to being in company, the main one being the social aspect for both horse and rider.

For a slightly nervous or less adventurous rider, riding with others may allow them to attempt rides that they wouldn't do on their own. Horses too, will take obstacles on in a group far more readily than on they will on their own. Anyone who has ever been hunting or mock-hunting and marvelled at thir horse's new-found bravery and jumping ability will know what we mean!

Advice can be shared between members of the group and strengths utilised. One may have a brave horse willing to lead others through fords or past flapping plastic, while another rider may be very good at map reading.

However, there are a few things to take into consideration before you set off. These will prevent your fun from being spoiled. Be aware that not everyone may be aware of the etiquette of group riding (or may simply have no manners, or inadequate control over their horse).

Before setting off:
- If possible and it's a large group, try introducing the horses to each other in smaller groups beforehand to make sure they get on.
- Make sure you all have similar ideas about the speed of the ride. There's no point in getting an hour down the road to find out that one person was expecting to walk and another wanting to canter.
- If your horse is uncomfortable being crowded and likely to kick, you can tie a red ribbon to his tail. (Not everyone may know what this means, so you still need to pay attention). Riders on novice horses sometimes put a green ribbon in their horse's tail.
- The leader or organiser should be made aware of any novice horses or novice riders in the group.

At the start:
- Make sure everyone is mounted and ready, with their tack adjusted. There is nothing worse than having one foot in the stirrup when the whole gang sets off!
- Set off at a walk. No racing starts please – they wind up the horses and may frighten other riders.

On the ride:

- Always ride at the speed of the weakest/slowest rider.

- Keep a safe distance from other horses. Nips and kicks can happen quickly – even if a horse has never done it before.

- If you're in the lead, make sure the whole group is ready to change speed faster or slower to save anyone being left behind doing up a girth or pile-ups when stopping!

- If passing other horses and riders, it's polite to ask if this is ok. Leave plenty of room.

- When dealing with gateways and road crossings make sure that all the horses are together as a group. This will prevent horses being stressed about being left behind.

- Wait at the top or bottom of hills until everyone arrives (if there is plenty of room to do so safely).

- Horses have a pecking order. Some are born leaders and some are followers. Try to be sensitive to this and understand that not all horses are suited to being at the back of the pack and some unsuited to being at the front.

- Ideally the leader should identify someone experienced to ride at the back of the pack, to help those in difficulty and to make sure no-one falls behind.

- Be prepared for other riders to bump and crowd you, take off without warning, or stop suddenly.

- If you are planning on camping or staying overnight you need to know that your horses will turn out together without fuss or argument. Ideally, try it at home first and keep an eye out for any bullying or potential fights or be prepared to separate horses into smaller corrals.

It's good practice, if riding with strangers, for each member of the party to give the leader details of an emergency contact, should they get ill or injured. The details should also include someone who can collect the horse, if the rider has travelled to the venue alone.

Riding Alone

DON'T DO IT. Hey, just kidding! Riding alone can bring many pleasures – peace and quiet, the chance to daydream, enjoy the countryside, and simply enjoy being with your horse.

Riding alone means you can make *all* the decisions – about the speed and the route, how long to stop for lunch and whether you want to make an extra loop.

Some riders don't really have any option when it comes to riding solo – perhaps everyone else at your yard has a dressage fixation, or you don't have anyone to ride with near where you live, or who can take time off to join you on your riding holiday.

However, if you are riding alone, whether by choice or necessity, you are naturally more vulnerable if things go wrong, and it's sensible to take some precautionary measures:

- Carry a mobile phone (if you've got one and it works where you're riding).

- Carry some means of identification, with emergency contact numbers. We sincerely hope you're not going to be found unconscious, but just in case… Even if your injuries are minor, if you're in shock (see next chapter) remembering your partner's name can be a challenge, never mind their mobile number.

- Leave your route and expected time of return with someone you know (and be certain to let them know you've got back safely).

- Carry essential items on you in pockets or a bumbag, not attached to the horse, in case you get separated.

Naturally, if you know your horse is very inexperienced or has behavioural issues, you should be a little more cautious and plan safe routes for the time being.

Further and Higher - Including Camping

- Riding further and higher needs more preparation: fitness, route planning, and gear. Take advice from people who know the terrain.

- Always allow time for unexpected difficulties or obstructions. It's usually better to plan shorter days with an optional extra loop if time and enthusiasm allows.

- Be prepared for bad weather - have appropriate clothing and emergency rations, and check weather forecasts before setting off.

- If you're planning to camp, try it out near home fiirst so that you (and your horse) are familiar with the gear. Show consideration for others when camping.

- Apply common sense when crossing water or boggy ground. If in doubt, find another way round.

- Riding alone or in a group are both wonderful - if you're prepared.

Coping With Emergencies 10

As off-road riding enthusiasts ourselves, we are the last people to put a dampener on your excitement, but emergencies unfortunately can happen. Knowing what to do if you find yourself in trouble is part of the preparation for your trip.

Much of the pleasure of riding through the countryside is getting away from so-called 'civilised' society: the downside of this is that you will be reliant on your own resources, and those of your companions.

This doesn't mean that you shouldn't be considering a journey without a vet, full paramedic assistance and preferably a helicopter on standby! What it does mean is having a realistic notion of what can go wrong, and what you can do about it.

This chapter looks at possible problems: some minor, some less so, and offers some practical solutions. Many can be resolved with a little planning and forethought (for example, having the right equipment with you); for others, you may need outside help and we suggest how to best locate it.

The purpose of this chapter is NOT to terrify you! Rather, it is intended to give you confidence that you can cope - admirably. We have ridden many thousands of miles off-road with remarkably few problems: however, it's always best to 'BE PREPARED'...

Disaster strikes...

- You are around half way through your day and your horse suddenly goes lame. You don't really know where you are on your map and not sure who to contact.

- You take ill yourself, this time on a longer trip. How long do you allow yourself to be ill before you think about getting help and do you know how to look after yourself in the meantime?

- Your horse takes fright when you are leading him, gets loose and canters off. In his panic he doesn't stop quickly enough at a gate, slides into it and gets stuck. You are unable to free him yourself. Do you know who to call or how to get help?

- Your ride includes quite a few river crossings. When you set off the rain is light and the rivers are low enough to cross. As the day goes on the rain gets heavier and the rivers dangerously deep in front of you. There is no going back as the rivers you have already crossed have also swollen. Do you know your alternative routes or how and where to set up emergency camp?

General points

- **First aid.** It is seriously advisable to have some training in first aid - a good winter project, perhaps, when there's less time for riding! Basic training means you can help yourself, a friend, or even your horse. At the time of writing, the BHS is running first aid courses with specific reference to riders, but any reputable first aid course will be of benefit.

- **Mobile phones.** Firstly, DO NOT RELY ON MOBILE PHONES WORKING. If you do have a signal, dial 999. In the UK, dialling 112 will pick up any available network, even if your own network has no signal. You may improve your chance of coverage by climbing to higher ground, if this is possible. In some situations, you may be able to text even if there is not enough signal to phone.

- **Emergency services** are exactly that - services for emergencies. They are *not* there because you are late, tired or hungry. In the hills they are often staffed by volunteers. They are there to deal with life-threatening situations, including serious illness and injury. Statistics suggest two-thirds of call-outs to mountain rescue organisations are due to poor navigation combined with inadequate equipment. Don't be part of this year's statistics!

- **Travelling in a group.** If you are in a group and there is a situation that requires help then the plan should be fully discussed *before* people head off. This helps to ensure that everyone is accounted for and that no-one is lost as a result of poor communication.

- **Help for your horse.** Bear in mind that if you are near a farm with livestock then they are likely to have the number of a local vet.

- **Emergency kit.** Have your first aid kit, torch, and whistle somewhere you can easily access them.

- **Route planning.** Always tell someone where you are going, what route you plan to take and when you expect to arrive. **LET THEM KNOW WHEN YOU'VE RETURNED SAFELY TOO.**

- **When route planning, be alert for possible short cuts.** When you're actually riding, try to be aware whether riding on or turning back will bring you to help more quickly.

- **Don't forget to pack your brain! A cool head and a thoughtful, systematic approach will help you deal with most problems.**

HORSE EMERGENCIES

You're in Charge

Good horse management knowledge is a must before heading out on your own with a horse. If you're not absolutely sure of your competence, consider enrolling for one of the many stable management courses (often run through local colleges or riding clubs) or courses run by the British Horse Society: e.g. The Horse Owner's Certificate. These classes usually include bandaging of wounds, recognising lameness, what to have in your horse's first aid kit and other good stuff to know.

If you're prepared, you'll feel much more confident at dealing with any of the following situations.

Lame Horse

If your horse suddenly goes lame, the first thing you should do is dismount. If you know he hasn't just fallen down a rabbit hole, then pick up the offending leg and check there's not a stone lodged in the foot. If the horse can weight bear and you know that there is a farm nearby (from looking at your map) then you can lead your horse slowly there to get help.

If the horse is seriously injured and cannot walk, you are going to have to leave him in order to find help, or send a companion (if you have one). Note that some horses may fret or panic if their beloved equine friend disappears without them: if you think this is likely to be the case, your riding companion may be better going off to find help on foot if it's not too far, while you stay behind to look after the animals. They will be more settled if they are together. Obviously, if there are several of you, this situation becomes a little easier: two can stay and two can go for help, for example.

If you have to leave a horse, untack him and try to secure him - either by using a corral, if you have one, or putting him in a field and shutting the gate. Never leave an unsupervised horse tied up - the potential for an accident is too high.

Removing a Shoe

Unfortunately there is always a danger of a shoe becoming very loose or twisted causing your horse discomfort with the risk of further injury. If you try to ride on with a twisted, very loose or 'sprung' shoe, there is a high chance of his foot being punctured by the nails or toe clips, or the shoe coming completely off tearing a chunk of hoof wall with it.

You are going to have to remove the shoe yourself and hopefully do this without causing any further damage to the hoof. You will have seen your farrier removing a shoe (if you haven't, make a point of watching next time.) Unfortunately, you are most unlikely to be carrying a set of farrier's tools - so you're going to have to improvise.

225

Removing a shoe in an emergency

See the photographs on page 142.

You will need a penknife (preferably with a variety of blades), your wire cutters, and a stone that you can hammer with, caveman-like.

• Gather your tools.

• Find a flat-sided, non-sharp tool in your penknife which you can lever under the nail clenches.

• With the stone, hammer the pen knife under the clenches to loosen and lift them. Use the wire cutters to cut off the ends of the nails if they are bent over.

• Lift the foot and place the foot between your legs (if it's a front leg). If your horse is an obliging sort, you could alternatively get him to rest the foot on a bank or a large flat boulder. If it's a hind foot rest the foot on your thighs.

• Start at the back of the shoe. With the wire cutters lever under the heels of the shoe being careful not to catch any of the horn. Lever under one heel and then swap to the other side and lever that side. Work your way forward from heels to toe.

• When you reach the toe pull the shoe straight off in line with the hoof wall to limit the damage.

• It's worth keeping the shoe by popping it in a saddlebag – when you locate a farrier he may prefer to straighten it out and re-apply it rather than putting on a new shoe, especially if your horse has unusual sized feet or wears any kind of remedial shoe.

If you have a hoof boot, put it on to protect the now-bare foot. If you don't have one, you'll just have to improvise further! We have used a heavy duty woollen sock doubled over (in dry conditions), or Duck tape works well – it's got good grip and is tough enough to protect the foot. If using Duck tape remember not to tape it to the hair on the pasterns or wrap it too tightly around the coronary band.

Loose horse

This can happen to anyone. Perhaps your horse was tied up and took fright, breaking away and running off, or took advantage of your immobility while you had hopped off to have a pee. Or you may be unfortunate enough to have fallen off. Whatever the reason - don't panic, and immediately make sure any other horses in the party are held firmly - you don't want them all disappearing.

Unless they are truly frightened, horses in general will tend to go back the way they have come, rather than forward into unknown territory. They are also more likely to rejoin the rest of your 'herd' once the initial panic is over, so encourage companions to stay still and together, rather than galloping after the miscreant, which will only make things worse.

THINK!

- **Where are you?**

- **When did you last go through a gate? Was it open or shut?**

- **Have you been past other horses? A loose horse will often stop when he comes to other horses, even if they are strange to him.**

- **Have you been near a road?**

This will help you to figure out your plan of action. Whatever you do try to resist running after your horse as this will exaggerate the problem, especially as being loose can make some horses very excitable. In any case, even if you're an Olympic sprinter, he can still run faster than you. If you can get to a gateway before he does to block off his route (perhaps by passing him in a wide arc or taking a shortcut) you will have more chance of catching him.

If your horse is tricky to catch generally, it's a good idea to always carry a treat for him on your person, not in the saddle bags which are galloping around with the horse! If he's calmed down and stopped running but is still being naughty about being actually caught, it may be helpful to ask your companions to move on SLOWLY and CALMLY in the hope that he will follow them and you will be able to catch him at a fence or gate.

Restraining a horse

If you find yourself in a situation where your horse is stuck and you are trying to restrain him ALWAYS be aware of your safety.

A horse which is stuck or panicking will be full of adrenaline which may cause him to react very unpredictably and can be very dangerous, even if he is normally quiet and reliable. He may bite, lash out or suddenly lurch on top of you in an effort to get free. We cannot stress this enough, especially as you , another member of your party or even a passerby may be feeling slightly panicky and anxious to help, and may unwittingly put themselves in danger.

And Go!

Always make sure you have good footing and that you are able to get out of the way *quickly*. If possible, keep another (calm) horse close by where he can see it. If your horse is stuck in a gate or a fence and is down on the ground but struggling to free himself, kneel on his neck if you can do this *safely*. This has the effect of disabling the horse and saves him from further damage, while your companion works to dismantle the obstacle.

If the horse cannot be safely freed (eg by dismantling a fence or cattlegrid), you will have to call or send for further help. The nearest house or farm should be found on your map if you do not have a mobile signal.

Contacting the emergency services

The emergency services will need the following information:

- The nature of the incident
- The precise location – ie grid reference
- Are humans trapped or in close proximity to the horse?
- Is the horse in water, i.e. a river, pond or lake?
- Is the owner of the horse present?
- Has a vet been called, are they on site already or what is their estimated time of arrival?
- Is the incident accessible by road vehicle? If not, is there somewhere safe to land a helicopter (sufficiently far from the trapped horse that he won't be further panicked?)

The British Equine Veterinary Association keep an up-to-date list of veterinary practices which have been specially trained in large animal rescue, in conjunction with the emergency services. This list can be accessed on their website www.beva.org.uk under 'Safer Horse Rescues.' If you are riding in an unfamiliar area, you may wish to check out this list for a local practice and keep their number in your phone for the unlikely event that you might need them. Remember, though, that *any* vet can help - it's just that these practices have undergone specific training.

Fatigue

Although this is a less dramatic scenario than the one above you still need to react as soon as you see the signs. These can vary from horse to horse and include:

the horse becoming uncoordinated

starting to stumble

228

flicking his head up and down

grabbing the reins and stretching his neck down

becoming unresponsive to the rider's aids.

Depending on the stage in the day you have different options. If it's around lunchtime, you should dismount and take the tack off for a while and allow him to rest, lie down or graze. You can take the opportunity to look at the map for a shorter route home. It may be worth considering finding a road - fewer gates, bogs and other hazards may be quicker and safer than cross-country. Consider finding a farm where you may be able to leave your horse while you arrange to get a trailer - it's sensible, rather than failure!

If it's later in the day and you are nearer to your destination you should again dismount, loosen the girth and noseband, run up the stirrups and walk home with your horse.

This scenario is particularly common with younger novice horses (who may have expended a lot of energy earlier on getting excited), unfit horses or elderly horses. As stressed elsewhere in this book, it's always better to err on the side of caution when planning a day's route.

Note: Fatigue applies to riders too – be aware of yourself and your own reactions and limitations.

Not lame but not 'right?'

This could easily be that your horse is 'feeling his feet.' Perhaps you have been riding on stony tracks for a while or the ground has been hard and rutty. Sometimes the signs are a lack of desire to go forward or the horse seemingly being awkward and not travelling in a straight line. If you see these signs, jump off and allow your horse to find some softer ground on the verge if you can. If the horse seems very uncomfortable then you should consider finding a shorter route home.

Cuts and Grazes

Simple cuts can be treated by washing the cut or standing in a stream to help stop the bleeding and get rid of any dirt, then cut away any long hair around the area and treat with a wound powder. If you are lucky enough to have found a clean running stream, or have a Travel Tap or similar water filtration system (see Chapter 11 *Further Resources)* then great, but if the only water to clean the wound with is a dirty ditch or puddle then you would be better to leave well alone and clean the wound later.

Major Wounds

Major wounds need veterinary attention. You can apply pressure to an area of bleeding to help stem the flow and find help as soon as you can. If there is an object stuck in the wound do not be tempted to remove it - you may do further damage or start uncontrollable bleeding.

Colic

Colic is unlikely to happen while you are actually riding but it can happen at the end of the day, and may range from mild, almost imperceptible signs to acute distress. Look out for signs of him:

- lying down more than usual (although bear in mind he *is* likely to be tired after your ride)
- getting up and lying down repeatedly
- standing stretched out
- standing frequently as if to urinate
- looking round at his flank
- repeatedly curling his upper lip
- pawing the ground
- kicking at his belly
- repeated rolling
- patchy sweating

If you see any of these symptoms than you need veterinary help immediately: don't wait 'to see how he is in the morning.' The vet will find it helpful to know:

- what his appetite has been like in the past day or so
- the consistency and frequency of his droppings
- what his water intake has been
- if he has had access to any unusual feedstuffs in the past day or so
- whether you've given him any medication.

If possible, try not to give him anything to eat until the vet has examined him.

Broken Equipment

Even with the best maintained gear, accidents can happen: your horse may step on a rein and snap it, or get caught up going through a narrow gateway and rip a saddlebag or pannier. Personally, we prefer that items do break under strain - yes, it's a nuisance, but better than a trapped or broken horse (or rider). It's not feasible to carry a full harness-making kit with you (even if you know what to do with it). Luckily you won't have forgotten to pack your brain, so it's a question of improvising with what you HAVE got.

Don't be stuck!

These are the items you are likely to be carrying which will help you patch things up for now:

Duck tape Don't leave home without it! It will repay you with myriad uses: taping up a rip in a saddlebag or replacing a broken clip.

Leadrope A broken rein or stirrup leather can be replaced temporarily with a leadrope.

Bandage (from first aid kit) – lots of uses for tying things together. Adhesive bandages such as vetwrap are particularly useful.

Strong string (which you are likely to be carrying to tie up your horse, tie up collapsing gates etc.) This can be used in place of a broken clip or strap or making an emergency halter.

Penknife – for cutting rope, string, bandages etc. If you have a multi-bladed one, such as a Swiss army knife, you can use a pointed blade or a corkscrew to punch another hole in leather

Don't forget other items which you or your horse may already be wearing – can you use his breastplate to improvise another strap needed elsewhere? Or are you wearing a belt (hopefully your trousers will stay up for now)? Tights are also handy – should anybody be wearing them (and willing to give them up!)

If your horse has broken a headpiece on his bridle, you may be able to put the bit up a hole – it won't do him any harm in the short term. If he's broken it at the top hole, you can fasten the cheek piece to the throatlash or noseband (if it's on the near side.) If it's on the off-side, turn the noseband round (so it fastens on top of his nose) and fasten the cheekpiece to the noseband strap. You may have to play about to make sure the bit is sitting level in his mouth. Alternatively, you may be able to attach the bit to his headcollar, using string or Duck tape.

RIDER EMERGENCIES

We've said it before (yawn!) but *please* do consider going on a first aid course. It will give you confidence that you can cope if you're far from help. If nothing else you should learn how to assess a casualty and resuscitation techniques.

It's outside the scope of this book to give you full first aid training - there are lots of resources for you out there (see Chapter 11). What we can do is give you some tips which will be useful in the following possible scenarios.

You or another rider:

has fallen off or been knocked over and is injured

is feeling sick

is showing signs of dehydration, heatstroke or hypothermia

has banged their head

If you or another rider have epilepsy, diabetes, asthma, severe allergies or another life-threatening condition, it is VITAL that at least one other member of the party is aware of this and knows what to do in an emergency, including where to find any necessary medication.

Rider's Tip – First Aid

- Always assess the situation before reacting so that you don't put yourself or anybody else at any more risk.

- If you are dealing with blood and it's not your own put gloves on. These should be in your first aid kit.

- HELP! If you are alone, or alone with a casualty and cannot leave them, try to attract attention by using your whistle or torch, or by lighting a fire if you have no mobile signal.

Bleeding

What should I do?

- With a bleeding wound, add pressure directly to the wound and elevate the wound above the heart.

- If the bleeding is profuse and will not stop then this is an emergency and you will have to seek outside help.

- If the bleeding does stop: clean the wound if you have access to CLEAN (filtered or boiled and cooled) water or a saline solution and cover with a sterile dressing. You can carefully pick out any foreign bodies which are near the surface of the wound, but don't attempt to remove any object which is embedded.

- If you are out for days and a wound begins to get red, hot and swollen then it may have become infected. This requires medical attention as soon as practicable. It is good policy to also have a tetanus injection, if the casualty's tetanus record isn't up to date or they don't know when they last had one.

- With any bleeding get the casualty to sit or lie and keep warm as the body can go into shock (see below).

Broken bones

If someone in your party has an accident, suspect a fracture if there is:

- severe pain
- bruising
- swelling
- deformity or if the limb appears to be at a strange angle
- if the skin below the injury becomes cold, numb or pale – this suggests that the circulation is impaired – this is an emergency.
- **If you suspect a head, neck or back injury, do not move the casualty or remove her riding helmet.**

What should I do?

- Broken bones are going to need emergency attention. Your priority is to arrange for removal of the casualty by the emergency services, and to keep her warm, comfortable and reassured in the meantime.

- Loosen any clothing which may be constricting the casualty as the site of injury swells - by cutting them if necessary. The only exception is a suspected broken ankle - in this case it's best to leave boots on to act as a temporary splint.

233

- Hardy hunting types often have stories about remounting and riding on with broken bones: however the risk of fainting and further injury, or further damaging the broken bone, is high and we don't recommend this. Someone with a broken arm, collarbone etc may be able to walk slowly for short distances if truly necessary.

●●

Concussion

Many riders have experienced mild concussion after falling off, hitting their head on a tree branch or even being hit hard on the head by your horse suddenly swinging his head round. Any of these may cause concussion, which is a brief period of unconsciousness, followed by recovery. The symptoms usually include temporary unconsciousness, headache and, often, a loss of memory concerning the incident. Vomiting and nausea are also common.

What should I do?

All head injuries are potentially serious, although an uncomplicated concussion is not dangerous and cannot be treated. The brain will simply need time to heal, and the casualty should be kept warm and quiet until they recover. However complications can arise in severe cases.

- Assess the level of response using the AVPU code (see box).

- If the casualty is groggy but responds to sound or pain, support him in a comfortable position and monitor responses. Handle the head very carefully because of the risk of neck or spinal injury.

Seek outside help immediately if:

- **the casualty has been unconscious for more than a couple of minutes**
- **the casualty, after having regained consciousness, becomes sleepy and hard to converse with**
- **the casualty's condition worsens after improvement**
- **the casualty has a fit**
- **the eyes have pupils of unequal sizes**
- **the casualty is losing clear fluid or watery blood from the nose or an ear**

With these symptoms, there is a possibility of cerebral compression or skull fracture, both of which require emergency treatment.

The AVPU Code

A is the casualty ALERT? Does he open his eyes and respond to questions?

V Does the casualty respond to VOICE? Does he answer simple questions and obey commands?

P Does the casualty respond to PAIN? Does he open his eyes or move if pinched?

U Is the casualty UNRESPONSIVE to any stimulus?

KEEP MONITORING & KEEP A RECORD

Shock

Any injury (or even a near miss) can lead to shock. The symptoms to look out for are

> rapid pulse
> pale, cold, clammy skin
> sweating
> The casualty may also feel giddy, sick or weak. If untreated, it can lead to unconciousness.

What should I do?

- keep the casualty warm. Lying on the ground is a great robber of body heat, so try and insulate her by using saddlepads, jackets or a sleeping bag, if you are carrying one.
- Raise and support her legs as high as possible, using the slope of the ground, saddles etc.
- Loosen any tight clothing.
- Don't let her eat, smoke or drink.
- Treat the cause of shock, eg a wound.

If the casualty continues to deteriorate, you will need to seek outside help. If she recovers and feels able to remount (ideally being led at a walk), watch carefully for any recurring dizziness which could lead to fainting.

● ●

Vomiting and diarrhoea

Unpleasant at any time, these are particularly nasty when you're on a horse. They may occur separately or together.

- Vomiting and diarrhoea need medical attention if they last longer than 24 hours or if there is blood present in either. Both can lead to dehydration and/or shock

What should I do?

In both cases sip plenty of clear liquids with a pinch of salt and sugar. Your body absorbs water best in small amounts so drink little and often and don't wait until you are thirsty. Your urine should be clear and straw coloured. When you start to recover try easily-digested foods such as bread or rice for the next 24 hours.

● ●

Hypothermia ("Exposure")

Hypothermia happens when there is a progressive fall in core temperature (below 35 degrees C). A hypothermic person may show the following signs:

Shivering and cold, pale, dry skin

apathy

disorientation or irrational behaviour (occasionally belligerence)

lethargy or impaired consciousness

slow and shallow breathing

slow and weakening pulse

In extreme cases, the heart may stop

Moderate hypothermia can usually be completely reversed: severe hypothermia when the core body temperature falls below 30 degrees C can be fatal.

How does it happen? Usually a combination of cool to cold temperatures, combined with wet and wind (not unusual in the UK!) Other factors, such as fatigue, injury or anxiety, can exacerbate the condition.

What should I do?

Move the casualty to a sheltered place out of the wind and rain if possible. Your aim is to stop her losing any further body heat.

Insulate her from the ground using saddlepads, jackets, dry heather or bracken.

Remove wet clothing - this robs heat from the body 30 times faster than dry clothing. Put as much extra dry clothing as you have on her, including head, hands and feet. Cover her with a sleeping bag or survival bag, if you have one.

If she is conscious, offer her warm drinks and high-energy food such as chocolate, if you have any. Do not give her alcohol - this will make the hypothermia worse.

The casualty should not be left alone in case they become unconscious.

● ●

Heat Exhaustion/ Heatstroke

It may seem an unlikely outcome, given the average British summer, but heat exhaustion and heatstroke can and do occur regularly. Untreated, they are serious conditions and can ultimately lead to death.

Heat exhaustion is often related to inadequate water and salt intake to balance excessive sweating. It is made worse by, for example, walking up steep hills on a hot day with full waterproof gear on (yes, people do.) Likely symptoms include:

giddiness or dizziness

fatigue

rapid (though sometimes weak) pulse

thirst

nausea

severe muscle cramp

Heatstroke (sometimes referred to as sunstroke) is very serious and must be treated as an emergency. The casualty may show any of the symptoms of heat exhaustion, but additional symptoms include:

- aggressive behaviour
- lack of co-ordination
- hot, flushed skin which is dry to the touch (ie, not sweating)
- deterioration in responsiveness, leading to unconsciousness

What should I do?

Move the casualty to a cool place - preferably close to running water. Get her to lie down with raised legs. Help her to sip plenty of water, with a pinch of salt in it if possible.

Wrap the casualty in wet clothing, or sponge her with cold water, which will help to bring down her body temperature. If there is no water, fan her. When she starts to recover, replace wet clothes with dry ones.

In the UK, heat disorders can usually be avoided by being sensible. If the weather is hot and dry, carry plenty of water and sip it frequently - don't wait until you feel thirsty. Try to avoid travelling in the hottest part of the day (generally early to mid afternoon) - if necessary, stop and rest in a wood or other shaded place.

Although you can generally find water in the hills, you can't *always* count on it, especially if there has been a period of several dry weeks. Small hill streams can dry up very quickly in these conditions. A water filter bottle will enable you to safely drink any water which you do find. and prevents you from having to carry too many bottles of water, which are heavy.

Wear loose, lightweight clothing which fully covers your arms and legs. Sunglasses will protect your eyes from glare.

● ●

ENVIRONMENT EMERGENCIES

Lightning

Being caught out in the open in a thunderstorm is a very frightening experience. Monitor the sky for changing weather conditions. Puffy white cumulus clouds, especially tall ones, are a potential danger sign. An anvil-shaped cumulonimbus cloud is a sure sign of danger.

anvil-shaped cumulonimbus cloud

The chances of you or your horse being struck by lightning are unlikely, but possible. You can't outrun lightning, but there are some sensible precautions you can take to minimise your risk.

What should I do?

Lightning tend to strike on mountain tops or tall projections (which is why church spires have lightning conductors). You don't want to be the tallest object around, as this increases your risk of being struck. This is the most important thing to remember, so that you can position yourself somewhere safer.

During a thunderstorm

- Ideally, take shelter in a barn or, if near a wood, position yourself in a stand of smaller trees

- If you are on a ridge or crest, move down to lower slopes.

- Stay away from water – river beds, lakes, standing pools or the shore.

- Stay away from solitary trees (at a distance at least equivalent to the tree's height)

- Avoid other tall objects, such as power pylons

- If in a group, spread out so you don't all get hit by a single discharge

- If you are in the open, get off your horse and tie him to a bush (not a tree)

- Insulate yourself from the ground by squatting on a pannier or sleeping mat. Crouch on the balls of your feet and don't touch the ground with your hands. If you *are* struck, the current will pass to the ground bypassing your major organs.

- Make your surface area as small as possible by rolling yourself into a ball and covering your head with your arms.

- Wait out the storm.

Rivers

Crossing rivers and fords safely is covered in Chapter 9 *Further and Higher*. The nature of the UK weather system, particularly in the hills, means that the flow of water is unpredictable: you might have set out in a gentle drizzle but by mid-afternoon the rain is lashing down, rivers are swelling fast and you're not sure if you are going to be able to get across the next one. This section explores your alternative courses of action.

And Go!

Crossing rivers swollen by heavy rainfall is never something to be undertaken lightly. The force of the current can easily knock you or your horse off-balance. In addition, rivers in spate may also be carrying boulders, branches or trees which can cause serious injury. Every year, people are drowned attempting to cross rivers.

What should I do?

Assess the situation.

- What is the width of the river and how deep is it?
- How fast is the water moving? (You can test this by tossing a stick into the water).
- What colour is the water? If it is brown or muddy and you cannot see the bottom, i it may be very unsafe.
- What is the footing like? If it is an established ford used by vehicles, the footing is likely to be better than if you are crossing elsewhere, where the footing may be bouldery or have hidden deep holes.
- What is the entrance (and exit) to the river like? Will your horse have to jump or scramble down or up?
- How experienced and confident is your horse (and others in the party) at crossing water?

One of the principal reasons people get into difficulties is the psychological pressures of making a crossing. After all, if you can just get across here, it's only three miles to the pub (or wherever). More gung-ho members of the group may be pressuring you to 'just get on with it'. Beware - this is when accidents can (and do) happen.

Alternatives to an unsafe crossing:

- Examine your map carefully. Where is the nearest bridge? What would you have to do to reach it?

- Is there a farm or other shelter nearby where you could wait until water levels drop? (Once it stops raining, water levels can fall just as rapidly as they rose – within a few hours.)

- If you are likely to have to stay out overnight, do you have the resources to make an emergency camp? Bear in mind it may take two or three hours to set up an emergency camp, so don't put off this decision until it's nearly dark.

- One possibility is to follow the river upstream, in the hope that you will be able to cross at a smaller tributary, or where the river braids into several smaller ones.

However, the wisdom of this depends on the ability of your party (is everybody feeling fit and strong?) and also the terrain: if you have to flounder through boggy ground, or pick your way along very steep slopes for a couple of miles, you may be better looking at other alternatives, especially if horses or riders are already tired.

- Sometimes you can cross at the mouth of the river, where it flows into a lake or loch. Rivers and streams are usually flatter and slower-moving here, although they will almost certainly be deeper, which will be an issue for anyone who cannot swim.

Because it can be more difficult to manoeuvre horses than people, a sensible plan may be for some of your party to look after the horses while a couple of people go to inspect alternatives on foot. They can then report back their findings, and is a more practical approach than everyone setting off, and perhaps finding themselves in more trouble. Naturally, if the party does split up in this way, each member must know exactly what the plan is and *stick to it* – you don't want people getting lost as night falls.

To summarise – river crossings are potentially extremely dangerous when water levels are high and the current is fast-flowing. Be certain that you have fully investigated the alternatives.

Dogs

Both of us own and love dogs, but there's no doubt that they can be a considerable problem out in the countryside, especially if - as so often seems to be the case - they are unrestrained by their owners. If only we had a pound for every 'he's just playing' as their hairy mutt comes running at you like a speeding barking bullet... He may indeed be 'just playing' but dogs have a strong instinct to chase, and horses have a strong instinct to run.

Please think carefully before taking your own dog(s) with you on a long ride - you love them, of course, but it's not fair to expect other riders or landowners to. Are you certain they are under full control at all times?

If you are out riding and are chased by a dog:

- Stay calm and reassure your horse. Do not get off.

- Do not try to outrun the dog – you will just encourage him to chase you even more frenziedly.

- Turn your horse to face the dog. In most cases, this will stop dogs in their tracks.

- If the owner is present, ask them (as politely as you can muster) to restrain their dog. We have found 'my horse hates dogs and will kick them' speeds things up. Some horses do indeed dislike dogs and *will* try to kick them or strike at them with a foreleg, so be prepared for this.

- If the owner is not present, growl at the dog and ask your horse to take a step or two towards them – often this is enough to encourage them to turn tail and run.

- Sometimes you will get a dog which simply follows you (not in an aggressive manner). We generally call in at the next house or farm we pass: these 'free–range' dogs always seem to be well-known in the locality and we have always found people willing to shut them up in a shed until their owners collect them.

Pass dogs which are contained in gardens or yards at a steady walk. Be prepared for them to suddenly hurl themselves against the fence without warning (much to your horse's surprise). Shouting at them to 'sit!' *sometimes* works. Be prepared for them to suddenly shoot out of an open gateway and nip your horse's heels.

Rider's Tip – Dogs

While your horse may never truly like dogs, it's a good idea to get him used to them during your training at home, by enlisting a friend with (obedient) dogs if you don't have any of your own.

Chased by Cattle

Cattle can be another common problem, although generally they are just being curious, rather than trying to attack you (but bear in mind that cows with calves at foot can be VERY aggressive). We've been told that certain breeds are grumpier than others, but we treat all cattle we meet with the utmost respect.

The biggest problem is being followed at close quarters by a frisky bunch of curious heifers or bullocks. This can make even quiet horses nervous, especially if the cattle are running, bucking and snorting.

The best laid plans…

Shonagh was teaching a novice pony to hack out safely – his first trip away from home. Everything was carefully prepared: a short trip by trailer with a sensible companion to a nearby farm, where the owners had been contacted and warned what was happening.

Having tacked up, the riders mounted and were leaving the farmyard past a cottage. Much to everyone's surprise, a farm collie leapt onto a children's garden trampoline and started bouncing up and down, appearing periodically above the hedge before disappearing, only to bounce up again a moment later.

After a startled look, the novice pony took it all in his stride. Shonagh however was in need of a lie down by the time they had (safely) returned home!

What should I do?

- Always pass cattle or other livestock at a steady walk. Going faster will encourage them to run, too.

- Pass cattle with the widest berth you can. You often find them lying on hill tracks where it's dry (or where they are fed by the farmer). If possible, ride round them in a wide arc, even if this means leaving the track (beware of boggy ground or other hazards.)

- Never get between cows and calves.

- If they follow you, resist the temptation to canter off. If they run after you, as they well might, the sound of all those galloping hooves coming after you may spook the quietest mount. They will stop following you eventually – once they have, you can then trot on.

- If you're cornered (which can sometimes happen at gateways), use the same tactics as for dogs. Turn the calmest horse to face them and take a step or two towards them. The cattle will step back too, which will allow the rest of the group to get through the gate safely. Someone can then hop off, hand her reins to another rider, and assist the last rider through the gate.

Loose horses

Sometimes you will come across loose horses, either out on the open hill or in fields through which you have the right of access. They will often get extremely excited at the sight of you on 'their' territory, and may gallop around, upsetting your horses, or may be aggressive towards you. Kate's worst experience was actually with a herd of donkeys with a seriously angry jack donkey, convinced that her somewhat bemused gelding had come to steal his harem.

We wouldn't willingly (or knowingly) enter a field of horses - sometimes, however, you don't know they are there until it's too late. If possible, we would try to find an alternative route. If that isn't possible, or you have come across horses unexpectedly:

- Keep walking – resist the temptation to gallop to safety

- Try to identify the nearest exit gate and head quietly for it if you think there may be trouble

- Give the loose horses as wide a berth as possible – hopefully they will keep grazing and not come to investigate if you are far enough away. This is often the case with herds of semi–wild hill ponies.

- If in a group, try to keep more nervous or excitable horses (or riders!) in the centre, or between other quieter horses and a hedge or wall where they will be 'protected'.

- If the loose horses come at you aggressively, twirling your long rope at them will give you a safe space (provided your own horse is desensitised to ropes – otherwise you may find yourself sitting on the ground). If you can keep them at a safe distance, you reduce the chance of you or your horse getting kicked or bitten. Hitting them with a whip is unlikely to work – you are too close and the loose horses are likely to kick out.

Help – we're lost!

Yes, it can happen, even if you've read Chapter 8 of this book. The best method of avoiding it is to *always know where you are*, by frequently checking your map and ticking off features which you can see. At the risk of sounding like your mum, *please* pay attention! It's so easy to go wrong by daydreaming or getting wrapped up in conversation with your companions - and then suddenly realise you don't know where you are...

Large forests are particularly troublesome in this respect. Not only do you generally have limited visibility, recent forest operations can mean that the tracks on your map bear little resemblance to the ones on the ground. It's easy to become disoriented and find that you don't even know which direction you're heading in.

Rule number 1 - don't panic. In the UK you are not going to be too far from a farm or road, and being late, cold or a bit hungry is not an emergency - at least for the forseeable future. You're much tougher than you think - your horse already knows how tough *he* is.

What should I do?

Don't just do something – stand there!

- Stop and think. Drink some water or eat a little food. These acts often give you a fresh perspective and help you better assess your situation. Bear in mind that if you are tired, thirsty or hungry,(not to mention a little panicky) you may not be thinking clearly.

- When you're lost, it's better to stay where you are while you work it out. A natural instinct is of course to keep going just a bit further, in the hope you'll realise where you are. However, carrying on may just get you more lost, as well as using up your energy. The exception is climbing to higher ground (if this is feasible – not if the light is fading or the weather deteriorating). This may improve your chances of being able to spot features on the land which you can relate to your map – and help you work out where you are. If you're carrying a GPS (and have a signal) it will of course give you your location. If you have an iphone or similar smartphone, you can also download apps which will give you this information (provided you have a signal).

- When did you last know for certain where you were? Find it on the map and see if you can trace your likely subsequent route. Is it feasible to retrace your steps to this position?

- Are you currently heading up or down hill? Are there any other features nearby (a river, bridge, building) which will help you narrow down likely locations on your map? Can you hear or see helpful landmarks like a road? Sometimes just turning around and looking at the terrain from the reverse perspective can help you work out where you are.

- If you don't feel able to navigate back to your last known position, mentally review your situation. Are you carrying anything which can be useful to you? Are there any hazards you need to avoid? When will it get dark? How does the weather look?

- Stay together! If members of your group begin riding around separately, someone will inevitably get confused and get even more lost.

- Emergency camp – if you are going to spend the night, do not camp close to rushing water. Its sound might obscure the voice of rescuers calling out to you.

If all else fails...

One of us – Kate – was saved once years ago by native pony wit. Caught out by a sudden snowstorm in near-whiteout conditions in unfamiliar territory, she turned her sensible Highland gelding loose and held on to his tail. After a moment's thought, Cluny turned round and plodded gently down the hill (following the one path she hadn't considered as it appeared to be heading in the 'wrong' direction.)

An hour later, they were both safely tucked up in the warm at a friendly farm. Turns out Cluny wasn't quite as lost as she was...

NB This may not be the technique of choice if your mount is a ditzy off-the-track thoroughbred! However, horses – and particularly ponies – often seem to have a good sense of direction.

Coping With Emergencies

- Being able to cope well with emergencies depends to a large extent on good preparation. It's good practice, before you set off, to ask yourself the following:

  What could go wrong?
  How can I minimise the risk?
  What will I do if it does go wrong?
  If possible, practise what you would do. Does it work?

- If in doubt on a ride, be prepared to:

  ask, turn back, find a short cut, check and recheck map, get off and lead your horse, seek outside help - whatever is most appropriate

- Time spent improving your horse knowledge, your navigation skills and learning first aid is well spent - if only to make you more confident

- Are you carrying the correct equipment, and do you know how to use it?

- If things do go wrong, keep calm. Very often a quiet thoughtful approach will solve the problem, or at least guide you in what to do next.

Further Resources 11

One of the great things about off-road riding is that there isn't a 'right' or 'wrong' way to do it — it's what works for you. Every rider (and their horse) is an individual, and as we said at the very beginning of this book, everyone's expectations and what they want to achieve is different.

An approach we've found helpful over the years is to keep an open mind: be prepared to listen to the experiences of others and to experiment for yourself. Think laterally — the very piece of equipment you need might be lurking at the back of the toolshed, or on sale at your local DIY store.

This final chapter is a collection of resources which we personally have found helpful: information, products, websites and books. Because currently there is not a huge amount of easily-accessible information for the off-road rider, we make no apologies that some of them are foreign (particularly American, where trail riding is very much alive and well) or that they come from areas not directly connected with horses or riding. Knowledge is knowledge, wherever you find it.

Some are directly connected with off-road riding, others have come about through exploring unlikely byways — both literal and metaphorical.

This surely is the ultimate joy of off-road riding — to see where a path may lead you. Travel well.

OFF–ROAD AND DISTANCE RIDING

Books

THE COMPLETE TRAIL HORSE Dan Aadland (The Lyons Press). Written for the American market, but some interesting information and some good trail anecdotes.

TRAIL RIDING Rhonda Hart Poe Storey Publishing (2005). Again American, but much useful and well-presented information

RIDING LONG DISTANCE Ann Hyland (J.A. Allen) Although aimed at endurance riders planning to compete, still much of interest.

Websites

THE LONG RIDERS GUILD www.thelongridersguild.com. Website for equestrian explorers with much useful and fascinating material, including historical long riders and suggestions for modern day equipment. The website (and Guild) founders, Cuchullaine and Basha O Reilly, have at the time of writing, just set off to ride round the world. As you do. They also run the **www.horsetravelbooks.com** site – a repository of tales of some incredible journeys on horseback, some jaw-droppingly brave (or foolish).

EQUINE RAMBLERS www.equineramblers.co.uk A long distance horse riding website providing information and support within the United Kingdom. Horse-friendly accommodation, trail stories, trail partners and forum.

BRIDLEWAYS www.bridleways.co.uk website promoting off-road routes for riders, with a members' forum.

AFINEHORSE.CO.UK Kate's own personal website, with hints and tips and stories from the road.

OFFROADRIDING.CO.UK the website for this book.

Chapter 1: The Ideal Travelling Companion

A PHOTOGRAPHIC GUIDE TO CONFORMATION Robert Oliver & Bob Langrish (JA Allen). If you want to learn more about conformation, this is an excellent place to start, with lots of pictures highlighting good and bad conformation.

Chapter 2: Equipment

EQUISAFETY www.equisafety.co.uk specialising in hi viz gear for you and your horse

HOLD-YOUR-HORSES.COM Suppliers of Spanish Zaldi endurance saddles

HORSE AND HARMONY www.horseandharmony.co.uk. Internet supplier of 'Barefoot' saddles and accessories, as well as natural horsemanship products. Personal, knowledgeable service.

PERFORMANCE EQUESTRIAN www.performanceequestrian.co.uk. A friendly and helpful mail order/internet distribution company, specialising in products and equipment for riders who love the thrill and excitement of long distance riding.

MALIBAUD SADDLES www.malibaud.com. Mmmm. Serious 'internet saddle porn' for the off-road riding enthusiast. Please ask all your friends to buy this book, then we can afford one each.

RADDERYEQUINE.CO.UK Equipment for the endurance rider, including Flex-ride stirrups and Hatrick hat covers

VETBED www.petlifeonline.co.uk. Vetbed Gold is recommended for saddle pads by many off-road riders - robust, easy to wash, bacteria-free.

Chapter 3: Where to Ride

There are many resources and websites listed within the chapter, but in addition here's some more you might find helpful.

Books

CICERONE GUIDES www.cicerone.co.uk Huge range of guide books all over the UK – aimed at walkers and cyclists but lots of useful information.

MOUNTAINBIKE SCOTLAND Kenny Wilson (mountainbikescotland.co.uk). Again, a good book for inspiration and we've ridden many of the routes (only seeing the occasional mountainbiker!)

RIGHTS OF WAY:-A GUIDE TO LAW AND PRACTICE 4th edition John Riddall and John Trevelyan (Cordee)

SCOTLAND : THE NATIONAL CYCLE NETWORK Harry Henniker (Mainstream Publishing) Many routes rideable on a horse – but check first. At the time of writing, negotiations are under way to improve rider access on cycle ways, but this will take time, and some still have barriers which will stop you.

Websites

ACTIVE EXMOOR www.activeexmoor.com Information on country activities, including riding.

COUNTRYSIDE RECREATION NETWORK www.countrysiderecreation.org.uk is committed to exchanging and sharing information to develop best policy and practice in countryside recreation.

EQUINETOURISM.CO.UK Visit for equestrian directories, area and riding information and specialist editorial sections. Promoting the horse industry nationally and internationally.

THE INSTITUTE OF PUBLIC RIGHTS OF WAY AND ACCESS MANAGEMENT www.iprow.co.uk is the professional body which represents individuals involved in the management of public rights of way in England, Wales, Scotland and Northern Ireland, principally as local government officers. Its members cover the whole of the field of access work, from countryside rangers putting in stiles to enforcement officers, path inspectors and strategic access developers, as well as those maintaining the definitive map and making public path orders.

THE OPEN SPACES SOCIETY www.oss.org.uk is unique in representing all categories of recreational user on all types of public rights of way, offering help to our members on problems relating to public paths - they can help you claim a path, remove a blockage, or lobby your highway authority.

PATHS FOR ALL www.pathsforall.org.uk. Path network development in Scotland - for access practitioners, community groups or just interested in outdoor access. They provide advice and support, publications and resources as well as training and useful information and links

VISIT SCOTLAND www.riding.visitscotland.com/routes/ offers a range of riding routes across the country.

Chapter 4: The Training Starts Here - Ground Manners

Books

ABC OF HORSE AND PONY PROBLEMS Josephine Knowles FBHS (JA Allen) A highly practical comprehensive guide to solving horse and pony problems, not just on the ground but also under saddle.

PERFECT MANNERS Kelly Marks (Ebury Press). Along with the other books in the series, *Perfect Partners* and *Perfect Confidence*, lots of hints to improve your horse handling, written in an accessible, fun style.

THE 100% HORSE: HOW TO CREATE THE GO-ANYWHERE, DO-ANYTHING HORSE Michael Peace, Lesley Bayley (David and Charles). Michael Peace worked with the Metropolitan Police Force to help train their unflappable horses. Sound advice on identifying physical problems which may be affecting your horse's behaviour.

Chapter 5: The Training Continues – In the Saddle

Books

CENTRED RIDING Sally Swift (Ebury Press). Improving balance and posture in the saddle through the use of creative imagery. One of Kate's favourites, referred to time and time again.

COMPLETE HORSE RIDING MANUAL by William Micklem (Dorling Kindersly). Excellent general guide to riding. Extra points if you spot Shonagh in any of the photographs.

FLEXIBILITY AND FITNESS FOR RIDERS Richenda Van Laun, Sylvia Loch (Allen Photographic Guides)

PEACEFUL WARRIOR WORKOUT Dan Millman (DVD). Kate's yoga teacher put her on to this four-minute (yes!) daily workout prior to long trips - and voila, no neck, back, ankle or hip pain. Very good (provided you actually DO it of course).

REAL RIDING - HOW TO RIDE IN HARMONY WITH HORSES Perry Wood (Kenilworth Press) Easy-to-read manual with many ideas for improving your horsemanship, balance and schooling. Especially useful if you work without a regular instructor.

SCHOOLING WITH GROUND POLES - FLATWORK SCHOOLING FOR EVERY HORSE AND RIDER Claire Lilley (J.A. Allen) Ever wondered what to do with ground poles? Wonder no more! Inspirational book.

Chapter 6: Fitness and Care of the Off-Road Horse

Books

GO THE DISTANCE – THE COMPLETE RESOURCE FOR ENDURANCE HORSES Nancy S Loving (Kenilworth Press). As the title suggests, aimed at the endurance rider, but an extremely thorough guide to conditioning the horse from the perspective of a vet and competitive endurance rider.The chapters on athletic foot care and conditioning principles especially helpful to the off-road rider.

Chapter 7: Using a Packhorse

Books

THE CAVALRY HORSE AND HIS PACK Lieut Jonathan Boniface (www.horsetravel books.com). First published in 1903, this somewhat dense tome still has much to teach the modern packer.

HORSE PACKING - A MANUAL OF PACK TRANSPORTATION Charles Johnson Post (Skyhorse Publishing) Classic text, written by a man who fought in the Spanish American war and ran mule trains over the Andes.

HORSES, HITCHES AND ROCKY TRAILS Joe Back (Kindle) is often referred to as the packer's bible. Written in the language of the West, it is a complete and often humorous presentation of the method of packing horses into the wilderness. Want to pack a piano up a mountain? Here's how.

PACKIN' IN ON MULES AND HORSES Smoke Elser and Bill Brown (Mountain Press Publishing)
Authoritative guide to traditional packing.

Websites

CUSTOM PACK RIGGING www.custompackrigging.com A Canadian company – but the pack saddle of choice for the serious enthusiast. Their claim is that they make 'the only adjustable pack saddle design in the world, built with the ultimate comfort to your animal and humane use in mind.'
TRAILMAX SADDLEBAGS www.trailmaxsaddlebags.com. Excellent, robust gear - we've tried very hard to wreck it and failed. Lots of good internet articles about many aspects of trailriding.

Chapter 8: Trying it Out – Day and Weekend Trips

Books

MAP READING SKILLS Terry Marsh (Pathfinder Guide - Jarrold Publishing). An introduction to map reading and basic navigation. A beginner's guide to map reading and using a compass, clearly explained even if you haven't done it before.

GETTING TO GRIPS WITH GPS: MASTERING THE SKILLS OF GPS NAVIGATION AND DIGITAL MAPPING Peter Judd and Simon Brown (Cordee). If you're keen to master this new technology, this is a good start, with lots of expert tips and learning exercises. Incidentally, Cordee produce and sell a whole range of outdoor books www.cordee.co.uk

Maps

ORDNANCE SURVEY
Great Britain's mapping agency. Produce a series of Landranger (1: 50,000) and Explorer (1: 25,000) maps covering the whole of Britain as well as digital maps. Their website has some good educational content. www.ordnancesurvey.co.uk

HARVEY MAPS
Harvey Maps www.harveymaps.co.uk .Produce a range of maps which are particularly easy to read and waterproof. The titles in the 1: 40 000 and 1: 25 000 series are primarily designed for walkers, but contain much useful information for the off-road horse rider, including the height, shape and slope of the ground in clear detail; the predominant vegetation cover; boundary fences; watercourses – the symbols indicating the width; buildings and other features to aid navigation; dangerous features such as crags or marshland. They also produce some maps specifically for horse riders, covering National Trails where riding is permitted. You can also buy a set of waterproof A5 route cards with clear maps and route instructions for the Buccleuch Country Rides.

Websites

LIVE FOR THE OUTDOORS www.livefortheoutdoors.com. Outdoor site with gear reviews
OUTDOORS MAGIC www.outdoorsmagic.com. Again, lots of gear reviews and active forum.
TRAVEL TAP www.drinksafe-systems.co.uk. With this you'll always have clean water to drink, for cleaning wounds etc.

Chapter 9:Further and Higher, including Camping

Books

CAMPCRAFT AND WILDERNESS SKILLS PGDrake (Southwater)

THE BACKPACKER'S HANDBOOK C Townsend (Ragged Mountain Press)

MOVEABLE FEASTS – WHAT TO EAT AND HOW TO COOK IT IN THE GREAT OUTDOORS Amy-Jane Beer and Roy Halpin (Cicerone)

MOUNTAINCRAFT AND LEADERSHIP Eric Langmuir (Mountain Leader Training Boards of Great Britain and Northern Ireland). Simply the 'bible' for travelling in the mountains. Naturally aimed at walkers and climbers, but with great sections on navigation, campcraft, mountain weather, and staying safe in the mountains – much of interest to the more intrepid off-road rider.

Websites

LEAVE NO TRACE www.leave-no-trace-training.co.uk Encourages responsible, non-motorized outdoor activities with minimal impact on public recreational areas. The programme provides education in outdoor skills worldwide.

THE MOUNTAINEERING COUNCIL OF SCOTLAND www.mcofs.org .uk. Don't worry, we're not suggesting you go mountaineering with your horse, but lots of information about Scotland's wild places and very good navigation section (and they run courses). Mountain weather information, frequently updated.

MOUNTAIN BOTHIES ASSOCIATION www.mountainbothies.org.uk who maintain simple shelters in remote country for the benefit of all who love wild and lonely places. Bothies in Scotland, Northern England and Wales.

TRAAKIT www.traakit.co.uk Suppliers of a satellite tracking service, which worked amazingly well on a recent thousand mile ride through remote country. Obvious safety features, but also friends can track your progress on their computers, and you can download maps showing where you've been.

ELECTRICFENCINGDIRECT.CO.UK Supply the corrals pictured in this book.

A GUIDE TO PLANTS POISONOUS TO HORSES Keith Allison, Christopher Day (British Association of Holistic Nutrition and Medicine).
With illustrations of the fifty most common plants poisonous to horses.

Chapter 10: Coping with Emergencies

Books
COMPLETE EQUINE VETERINARY MANUAL by Tony Pavord and Marcy Pavord
Tony & Marcy Pavord. A really good veterinary reference manual, examining every known equine disease in detail. Some excellent photographs.

DON'T FORGET THE DUCT TAPE: TIPS AND TRICKS FOR REPAIRING OUTDOOR GEAR Hostetter,K (The Mountaineers Books)

FIRST AID FOR MY HORSE by Anke Rusbuldt (Cadmos)
What to do in an emergency and how to make best use of the time whilst waiting for the vet.Includes bandaging, wounds, fractures and abdominal problems.

FIRST AID MANUAL: The Authorised Manual of St. John Ambulance, St. Andrew's Ambulance Association, and the British Red Cross.

POCKET FIRST AID AND WILDERNESS MEDICINE J Duff and P Gormly (Cicerone).

Acknowledgements

We sincerely hope you have enjoyed reading this book as much as we enjoyed writing it. Of course it wasn't just us: many people generously gave of their time to help and advise us, and pour us stiff drinks from time to time when the pressure of deadlines became all-consuming.

We especially would like to thank Mark Weallans for his inspired artwork, and Caroline Heard for the excellent photography. You have both been an absolute joy to work with.

Thanks are also due to:

Catriona Goulding, PG Dip Animal Physiotherapy, for her suggestions on equine massage and physiology;

Dr Morag Martindale, for her input on the first aid section for humans;

Mo Prior, superseamstress, for checking and correcting our sewing instructions for saddlebags;

Karen Walsh, BA(Hons) ASRM for helping devise the test for rider fitness;

Vyv Wood-Gee, expert on access matters and a brilliant off-road riding companion.

For reading the draft and making splendid suggestions for improvements:

Sarah Houston BHSI, Felicity Ivory BHSAI, Debbie Corbitt, Shelagh Steven BHSSM II. We couldn't have done it without you, but any errors are all our own work.

Most of all, we would like to thank Greg and Bill, for their unflagging support and for cheerfully getting their own suppers. Again.

Index

Index

www.offroadriding.co.uk